MW01608551

TO PARENT, GRANDPARENTS, OTHER ADULTS AND TEACHERS

Parents, grandparents, other adult friends, family members and teachers are encouraged to help the young marine engineer to learn about the pages in this book by working with her/him to review the drawings and the parts of the ship, and by repeating their names and functions. A short glossary is in the front of the book to assist the child (and adults) in learning some of the more difficult and unfamiliar names. Some of the pages are more difficult than others, but these have been placed toward the end of the book so as not to discourage the young reader. "Heating System" and "Cooling System" are examples of these. The more difficult pages are included to present challenges to the reader. Challenges are good and will make the reader ask questions. Questions provide good avenues for learning new things. It is important that you help them to answer the questions by guiding them toward solutions such as a dictionary or other sources of information.

Children who read and color the book are encouraged to name the parts as they are coloring and to think about the purpose of each part. Colored pencils are recommended for coloring as many of the parts are small and detailed.

This book is about Passenger Ships. Additional books in the series will cover Tug Boats, Fishing Boats, Ferry Boats, Cargo Ships and Barges. Ships and boats contain many of the systems and equipment which are essential to providing the necessities of life, safety and comfort and which represent examples of modern engineering achievement. If only one reader goes on to study any of the many fields of engineering, this book will have fulfilled its purpose.

**YOUNG MARINE ENGINEER'S COLORING BOOK
About PASSENGER SHIPS**

©2013 Peter S. Zimmerman

ISBN: 978-1-938883-27-9

www.pszimmerman.com

All rights reserved. No part of this book may be reproduced in any form or by any electronic or mechanical means, including information storage and retrieval systems, without permission in writing from the author, except by a reviewer, who may quote brief passages in review.

All drawings, photos and text are by the Author.

Produced by Maine Authors Publishing
558 Main Street, Rockland, Maine 04841
www.maineauthorspublishing.com

Printed in the United States of America

TABLE OF CONTENTS

GLOSSARY

AFT	The direction toward the back end of the ship.
AFT DECK	The deck at the back end of the ship.
BALLAST WATER	The seawater in the tanks which helps to keep the ship upright.
BINNACLE	The stand on the bridge, in front of the steering wheel, in which the compass sits.
BITT	The thing on the deck that has two posts, and mooring lines are attached to it.
BOLLARD	The thing on the pier like a big knob to which the loop in a mooring line is attached.
BOW	The front end of the ship.
BOW THRUSTER	The machine like a sideways propeller that moves the bow in and out from a pier.
BRIDGE	The room where the Captain and officers drive the ship.
BULBOUS BOW	The big bulb shape at the front end of the ship which helps make the ship go faster.
CABIN	A room in which passengers live and sleep.
COFFERDAM	A space between two tanks which hold different types of liquid.
DEPTH SOUNDER	An electronic device which tells the Captain how deep the water is under the ship.
ENGINE CONTROL	A device on the bridge which controls the speed and direction of the engine.
FAN COIL UNIT	A device in a cabin which provides heat or cooling.

FOREDECK	The deck at the front of the ship.
FORWARD	The direction toward the front end of the ship.
GENERATOR	The electrical device which supplies electricity. It is driven by the diesel engine.
HATCH	The opening in the deck through which cargo is placed in the hold.
IMPELLER	The moving part of a pump which pushes the liquid through the pipes.
MACHINERY SPACE	The space in the ship that contains machinery and pipes and electric wires.
PASSAGEWAY	The long hallway that connects all the cabins and other rooms.
PORT	The left side of the ship.
PROPELLER	The large wheel with blades that pushes the ship forward or backward.
RADAR	The electronic device on the bridge that sends out radio waves that bounce off ships and land.
REDUCTION GEAR	The big mechanical device attached to the motor that makes the propeller shaft go slower.
RUDDER	The large flat blade that is used to turn the ship to port or starboard.
SATELLITE ANTENNA	The electronic antenna on top of the ship that sends radio messages to a satellite.
STARBOARD	The right side of the ship.
STERN	The back end of the ship.
SWITCHBOARD	The box with lots of switches to turn things on and off.

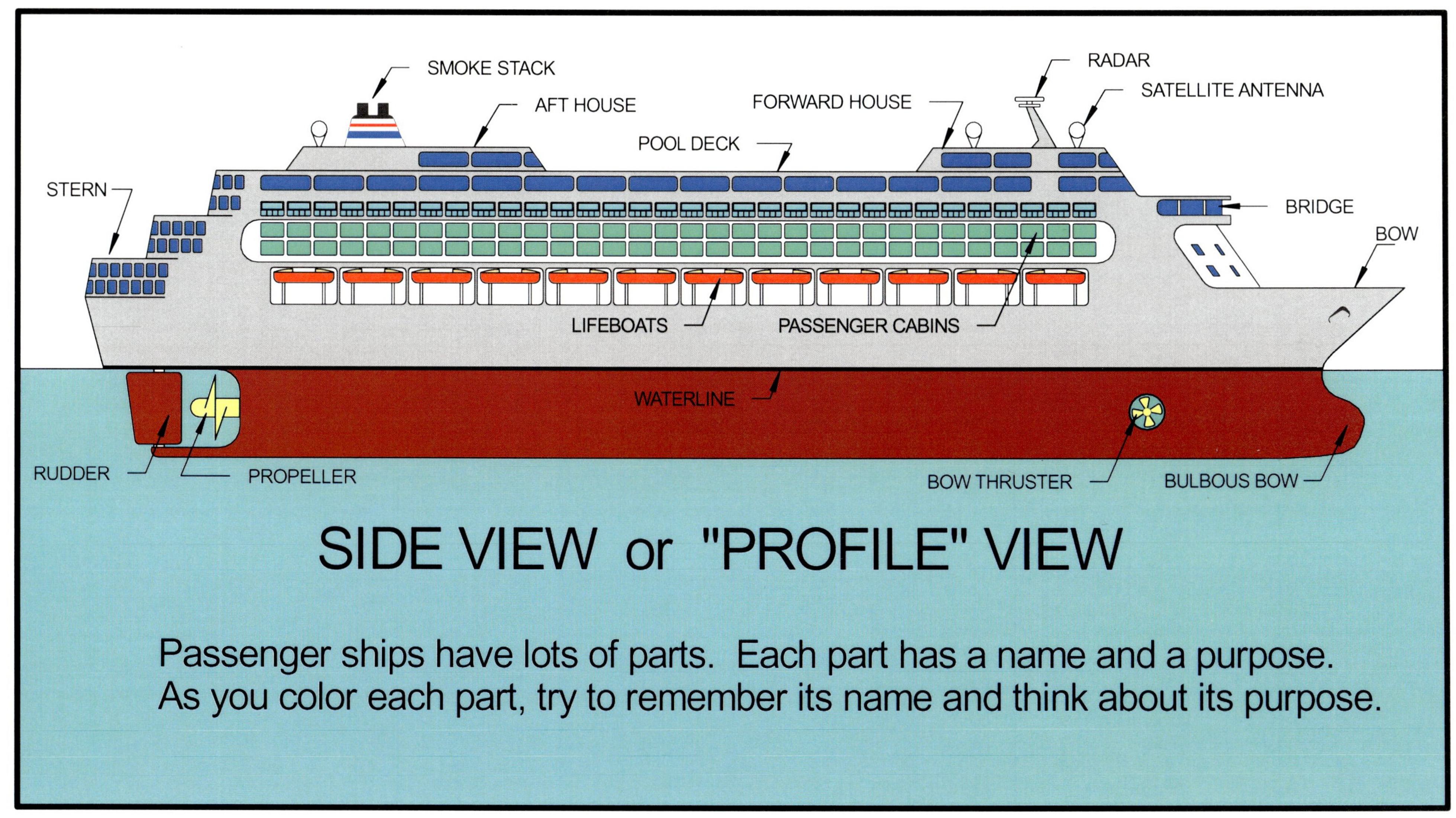

SMOKE STACK
RADAR
SATELLITE ANTENNA
AFT HOUSE
FORWARD HOUSE
POOL DECK
STERN
BRIDGE
BOW
LIFEBOATS
PASSENGER CABINS
WATERLINE
RUDDER
PROPELLER
BOW THRUSTER
BULBOUS BOW
SIDE VIEW or "PROFILE" VIEW
Passenger ships have lots of parts. Each part has a name and a purpose.
As you color each part, try to remember its name and think about its purpose.

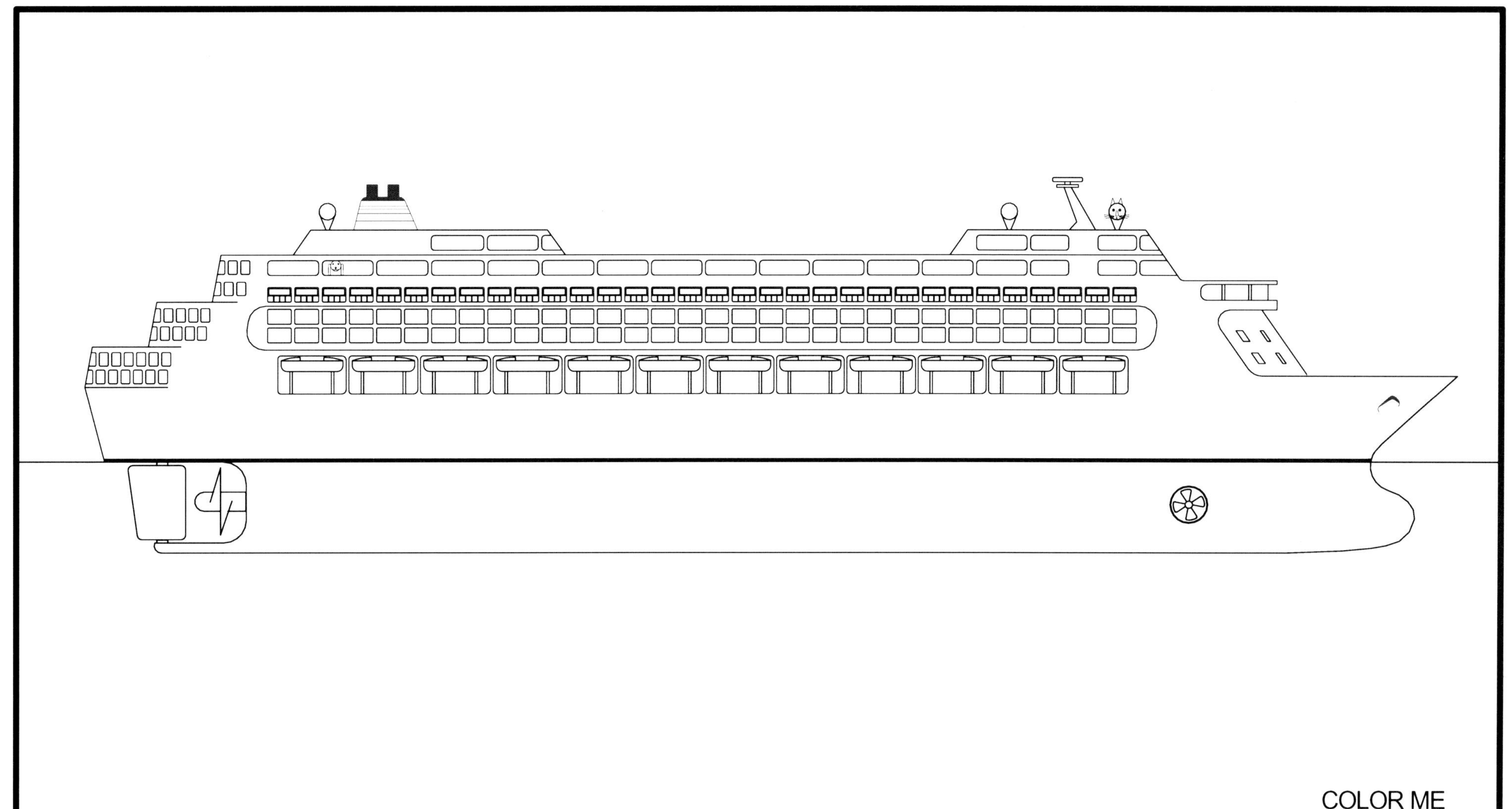

COLOR ME

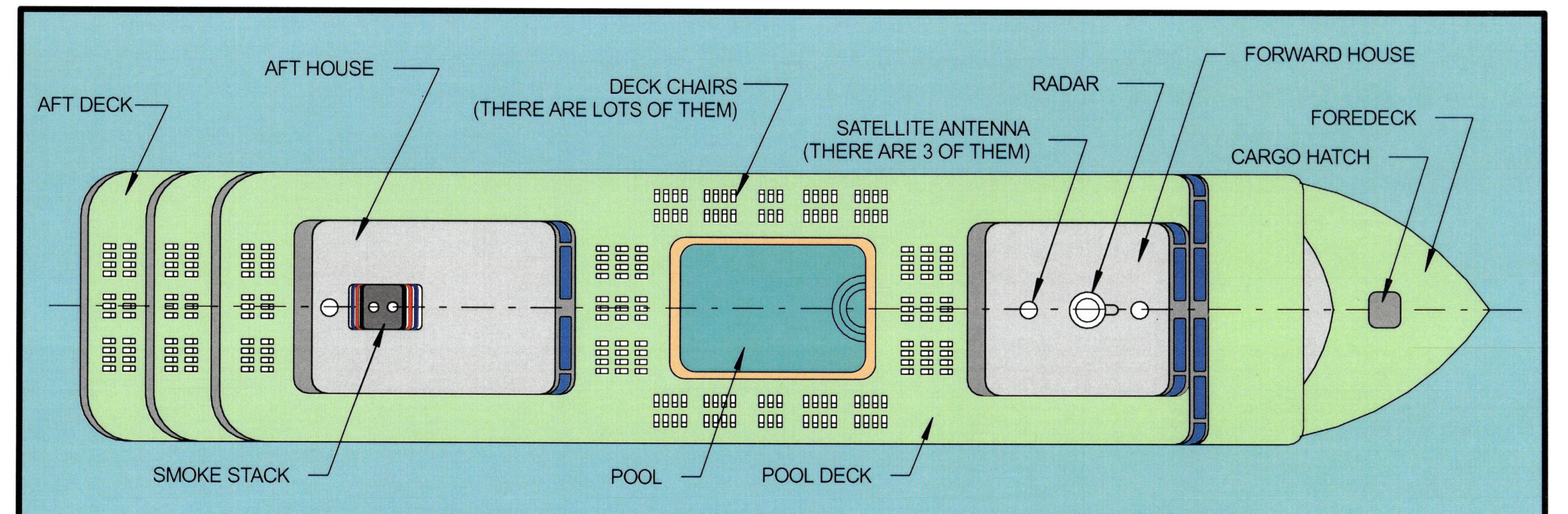

"BIRD'S EYE VIEW" or PLAN VIEW

There might be a gymnasium in the aft house
and there might be a dance floor in the forward house.

Food and supplies are loaded into the ship through the cargo hatch.

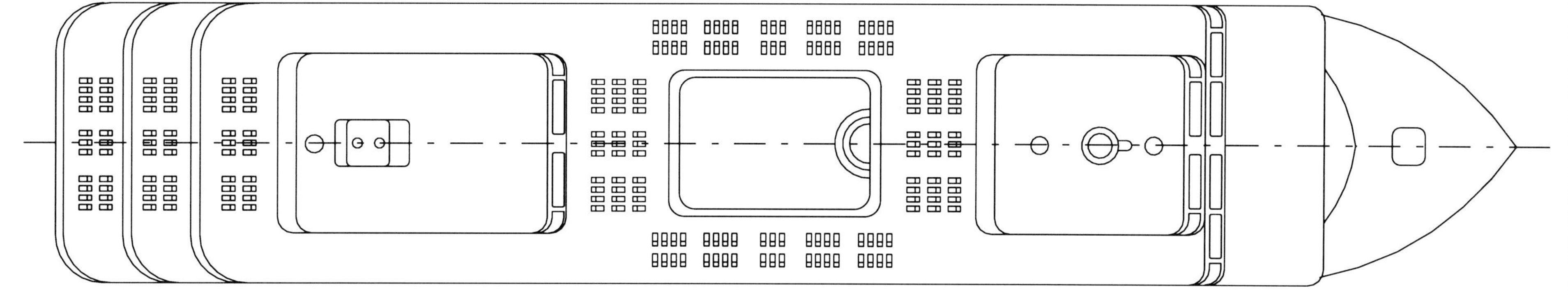

COLOR ME

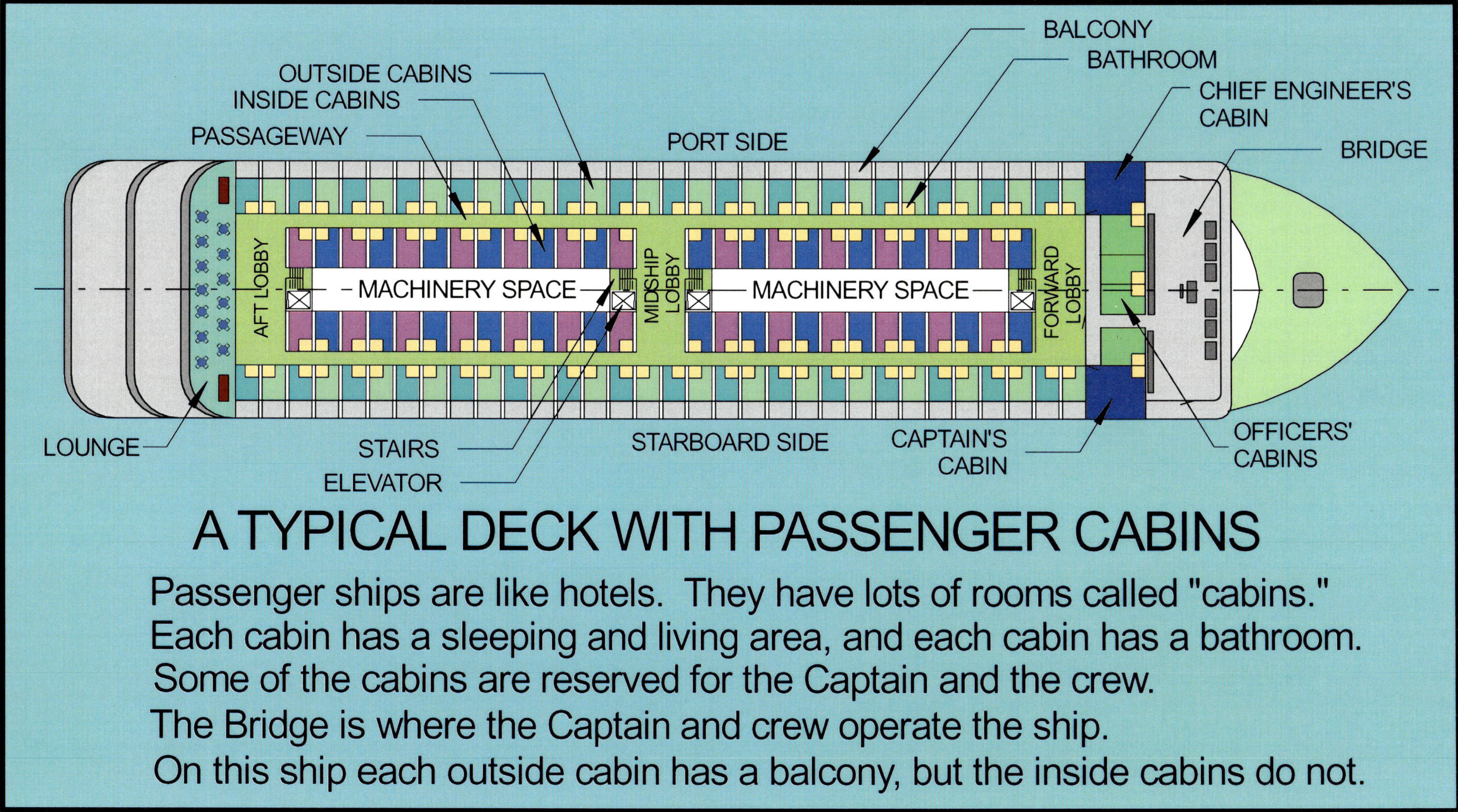

A TYPICAL DECK WITH PASSENGER CABINS

Passenger ships are like hotels. They have lots of rooms called "cabins."
Each cabin has a sleeping and living area, and each cabin has a bathroom.
Some of the cabins are reserved for the Captain and the crew.
The Bridge is where the Captain and crew operate the ship.
On this ship each outside cabin has a balcony, but the inside cabins do not.

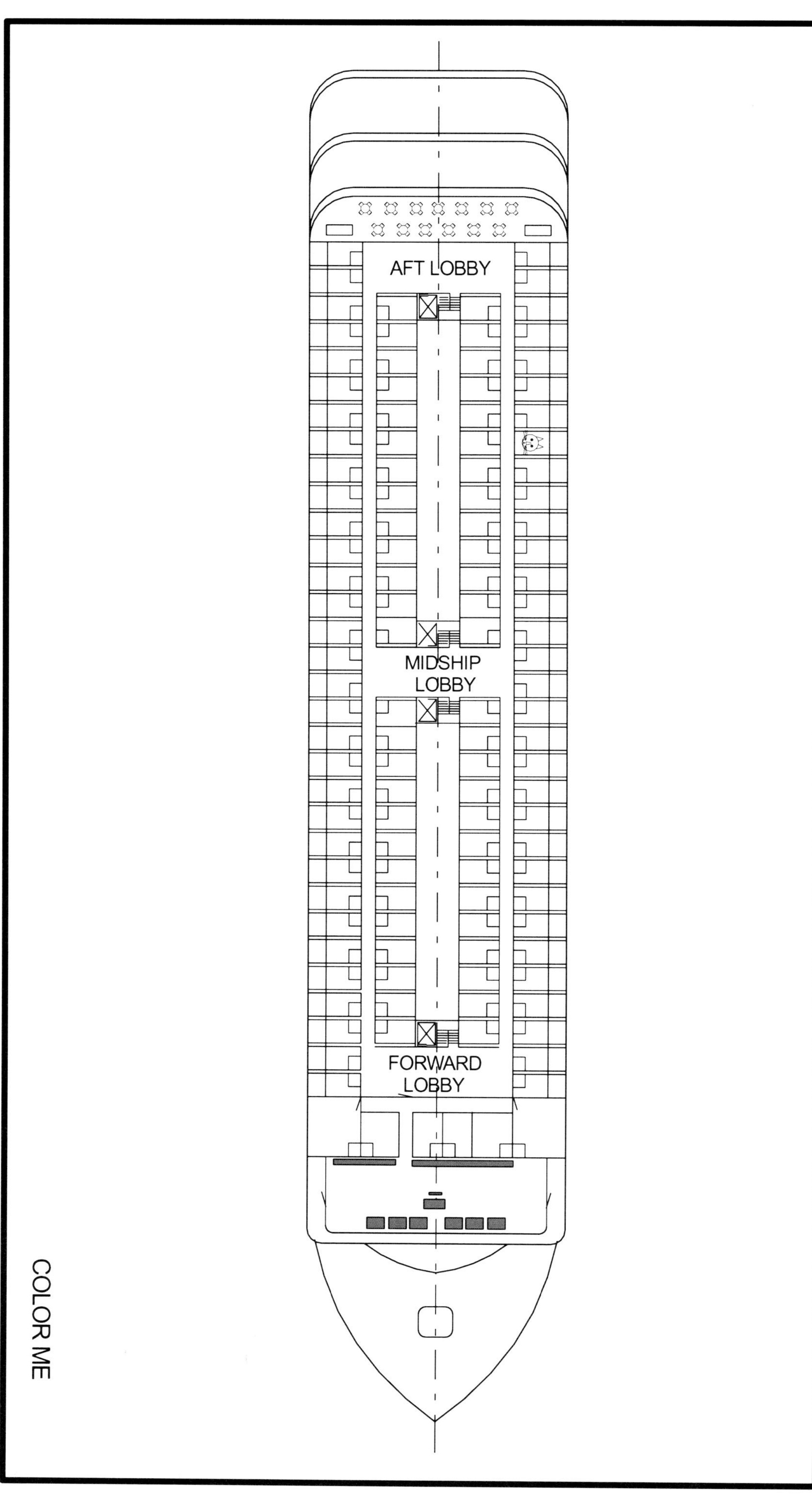

COLOR ME

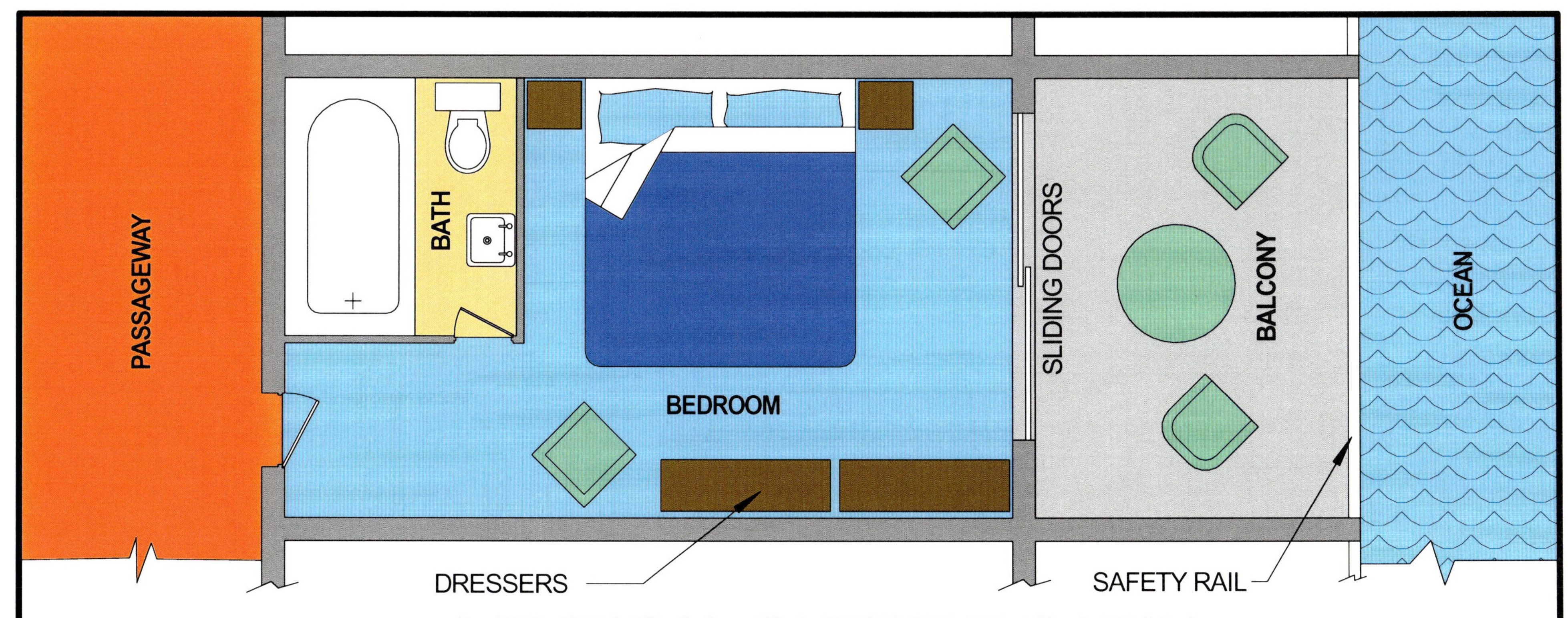

A TYPICAL OUTSIDE CABIN

An outside cabin has a balcony, a bedroom and a bath. The bedroom has a bed and two chairs. It also has two dressers for clothes. The bath has a tub, a toilet and a sink.

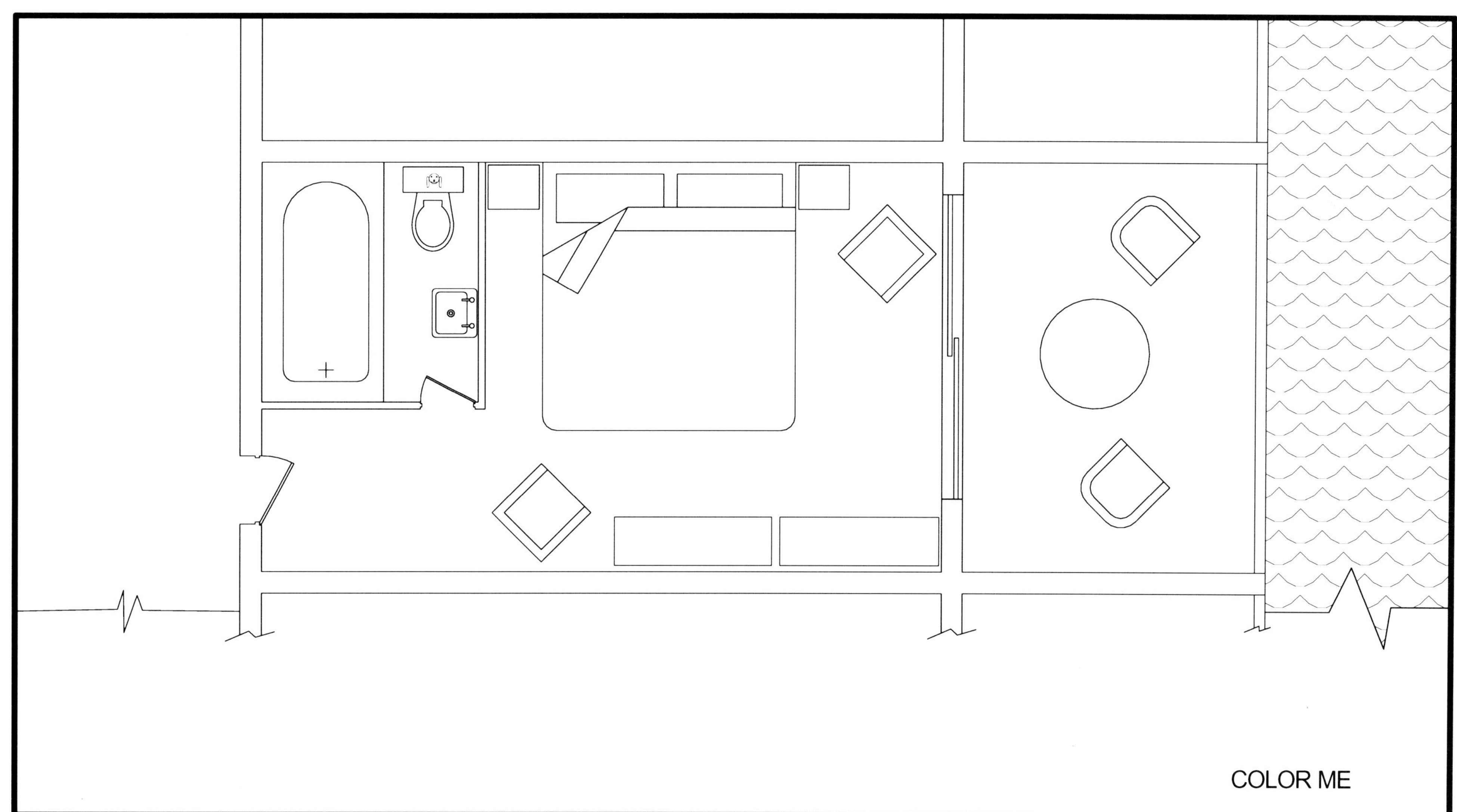

8

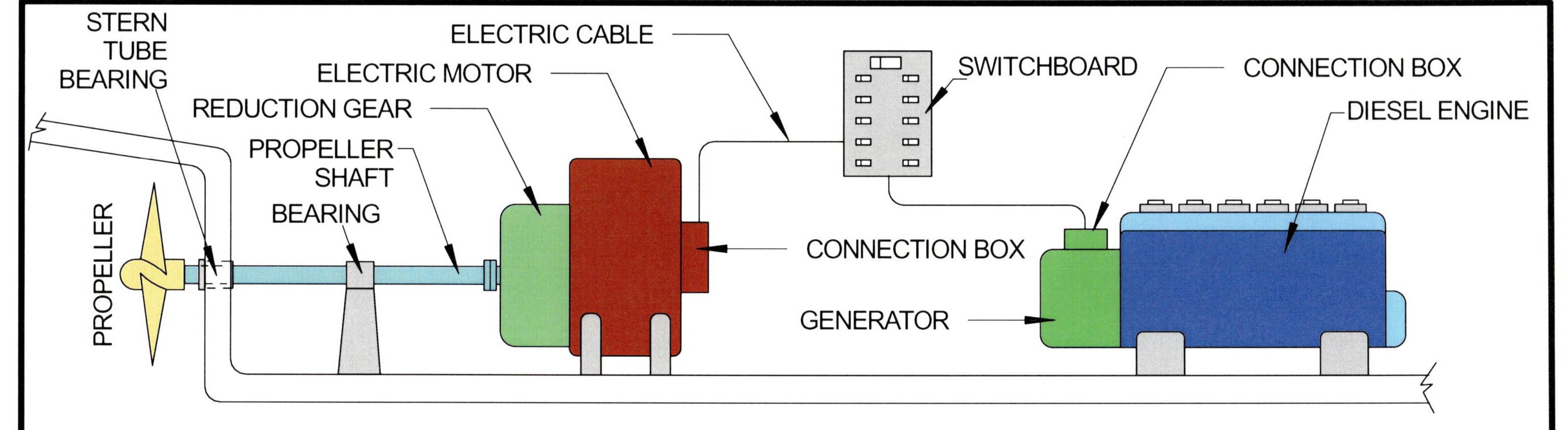

THE POWER TEAM WORKS TOGETHER

The diesel engine drives the generator.   The generator provides electricity to the electric motor through the switchboard.   The electric motor turns the propeller shaft.   The propeller shaft turns the propeller, which pushes the ship.   The bearings support the shaft

Between the electric motor and the propeller shaft is the reduction gear which reduces the fast turns of the motor to a slower speed.

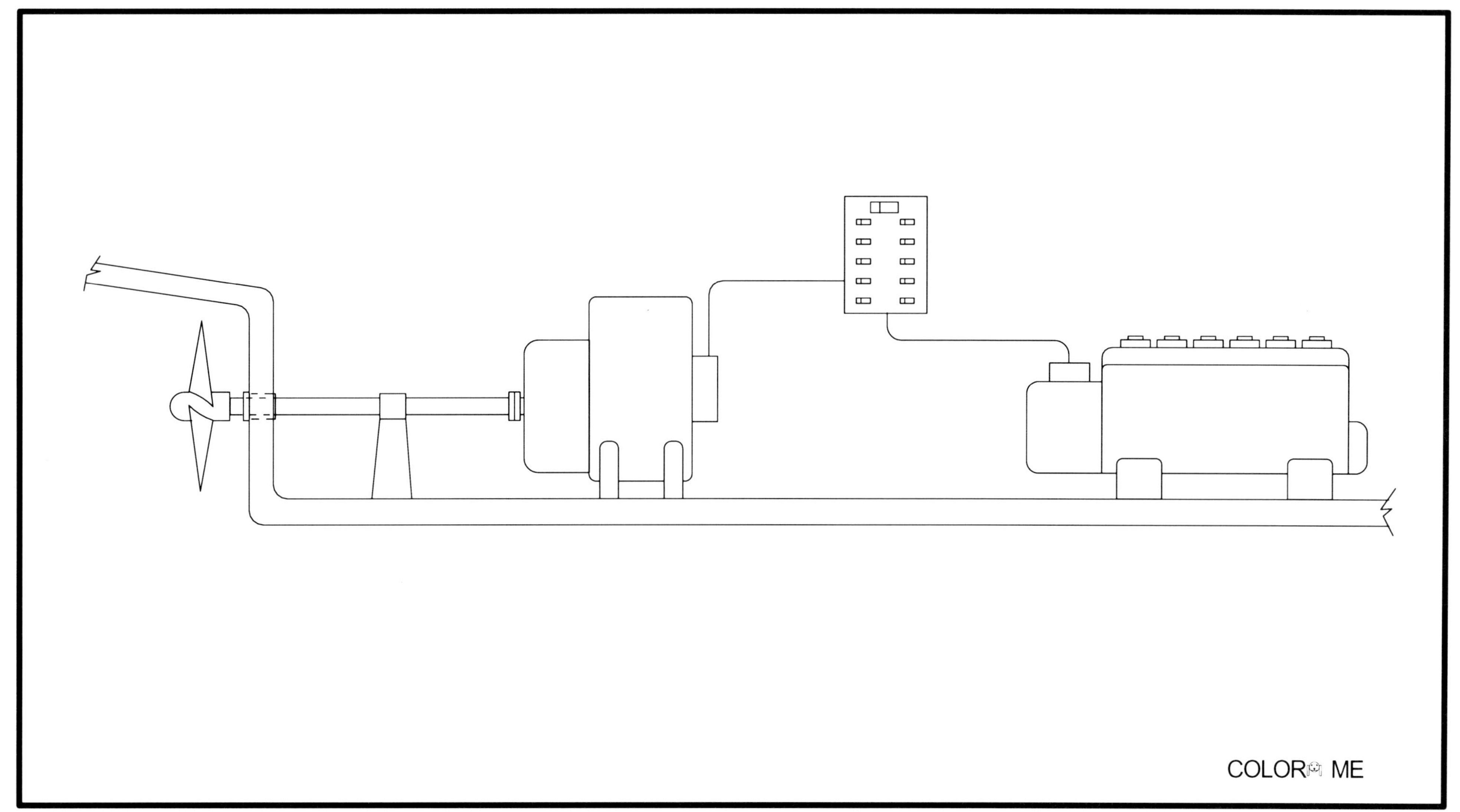

10

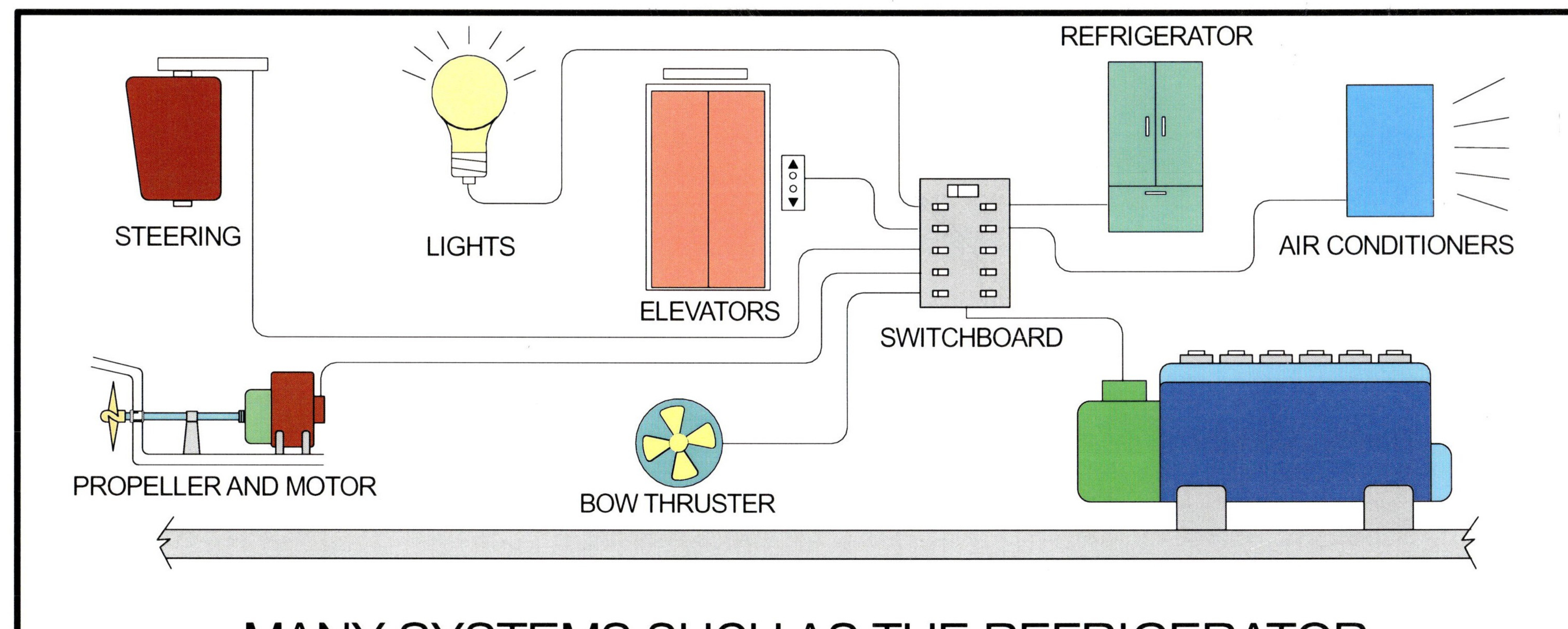

MANY SYSTEMS SUCH AS THE REFRIGERATOR
USE ELECTRICITY FROM THE GENERATOR

Which of these do you have in your house?

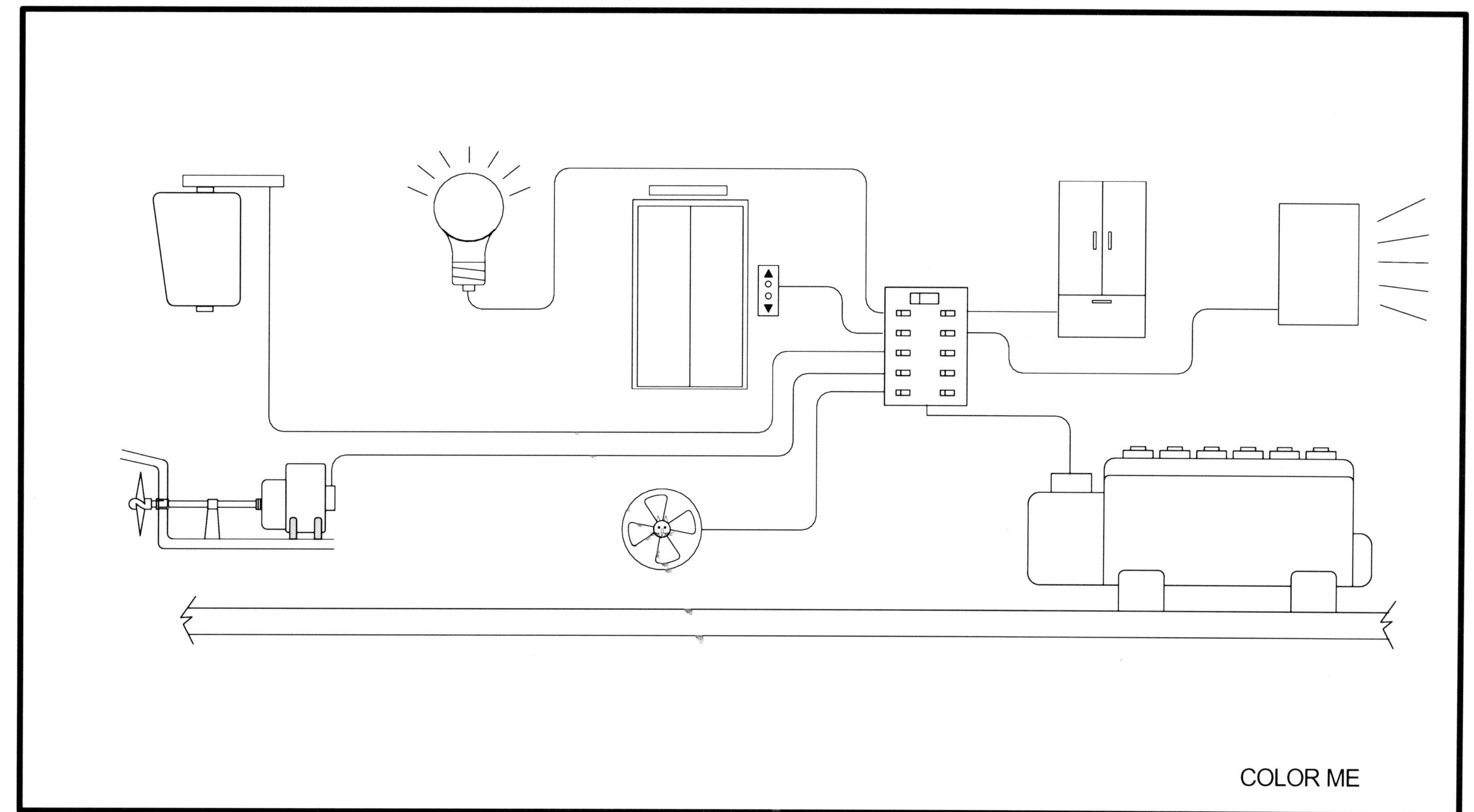
COLOR ME

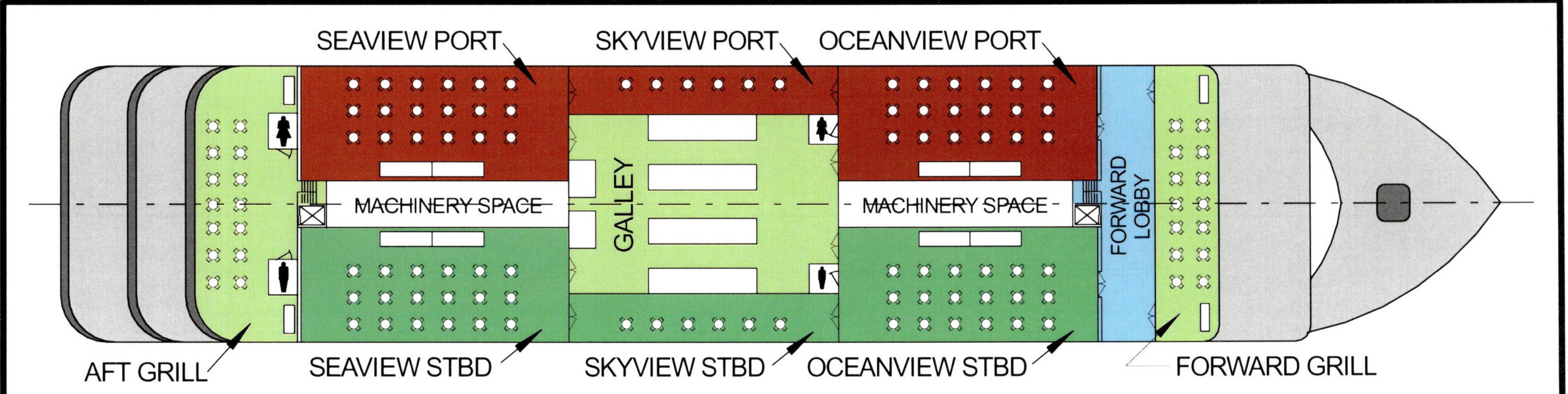

CUISINE DECK (WHERE PEOPLE EAT)

The Cuisine Deck is where the passengers eat their meals and snacks. There are lots of restaurants on the Cuisine Deck.

The Port Side is the left side of the ship. The Starboard Side is the right side of the ship. STBD means Starboard. Can you guess how they named the restaurants?

There are two ladies rooms and two mens rooms. Can you find them?

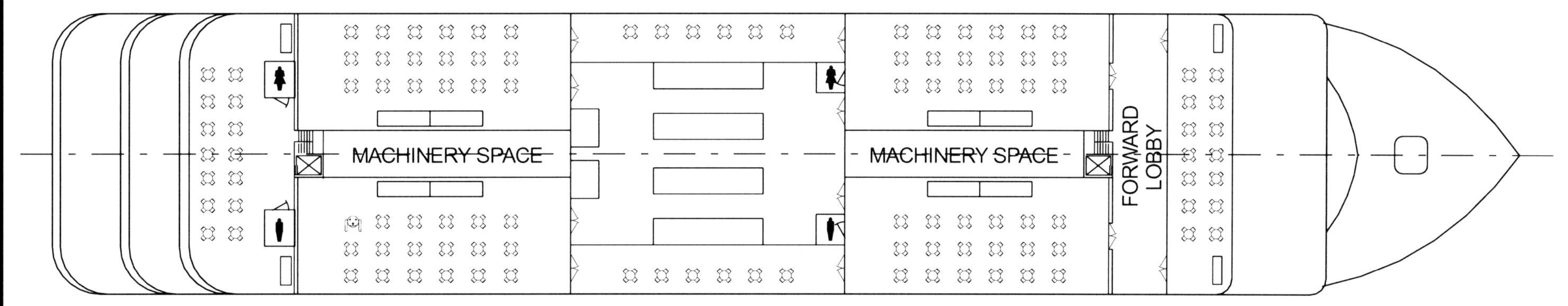

COLOR ME

14

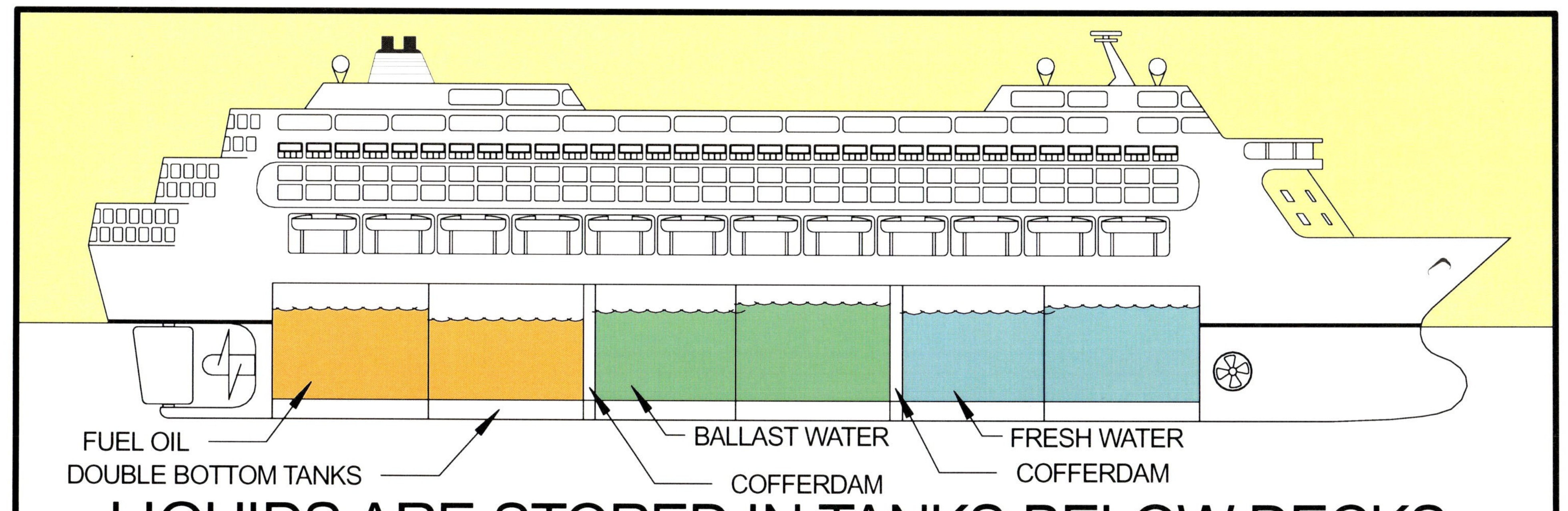

LIQUIDS ARE STORED IN TANKS BELOW DECKS

Fresh water tanks hold drinking water and bath water.   Ballast water in the ballast tanks is used to keep the ship upright by adding weight in the bottom of the ship. The fuel oil is to feed the diesel engine and the boilers.

Cofferdams are empty spaces between tanks of different liquids. Their purpose is to prevent one type of liquid from leaking into a tank with a different liquid.

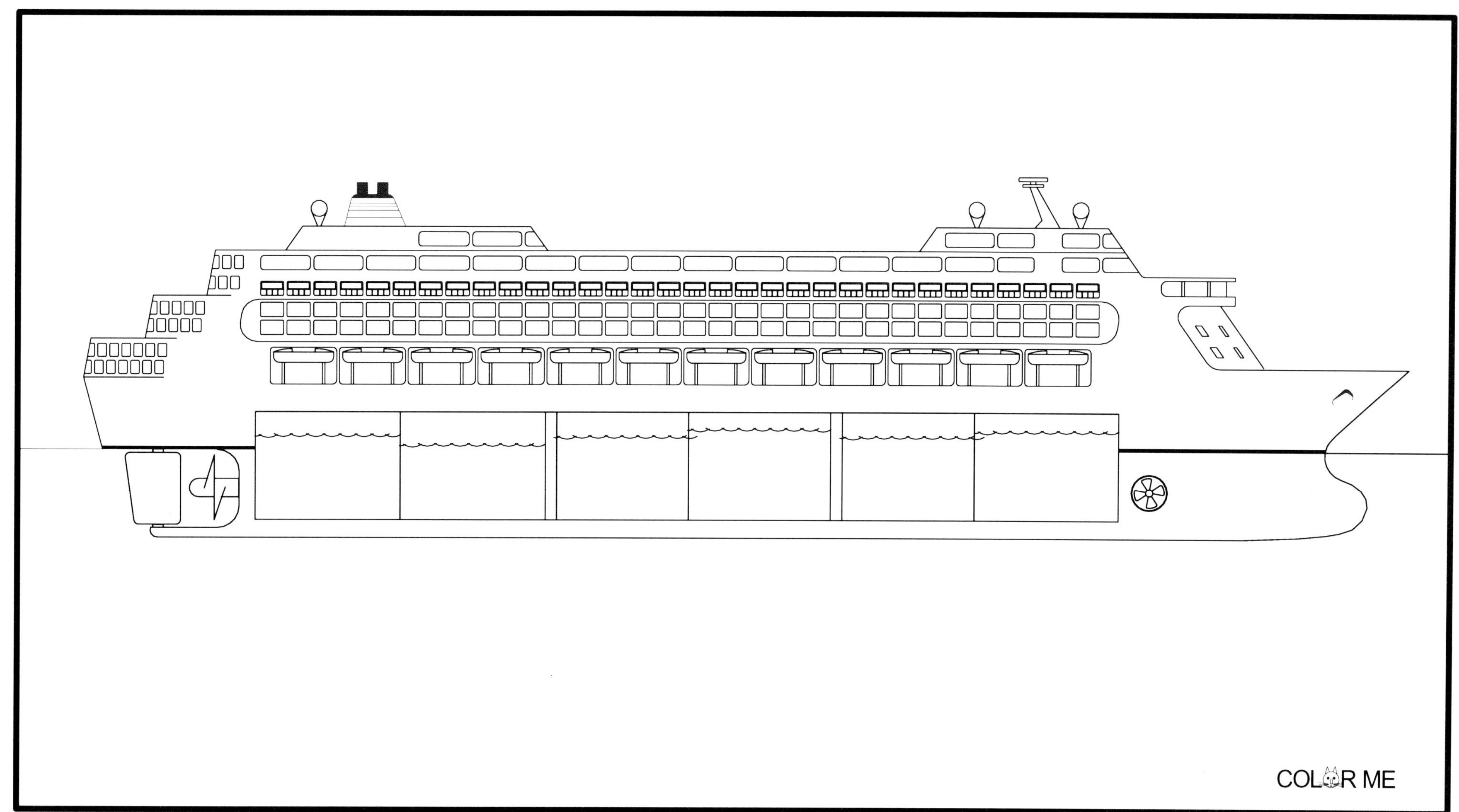
COLOR ME

CROSS SECTION THROUGH THE SHIP

A cross section is what you would see if you made an imaginary cut through the ship.

Can you find the passageways between the inside and outside cabins?

Often the double bottom tanks are not filled.

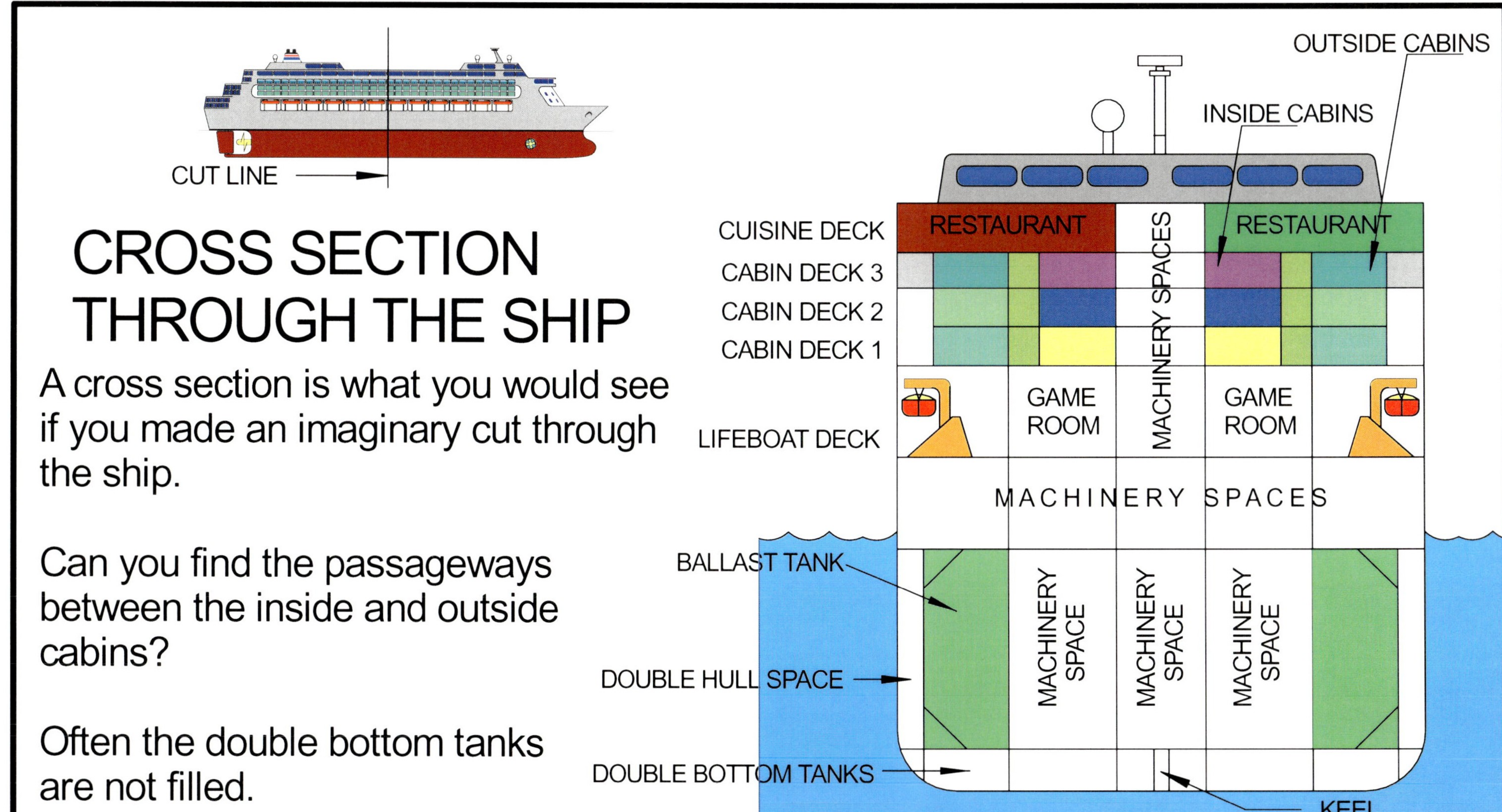

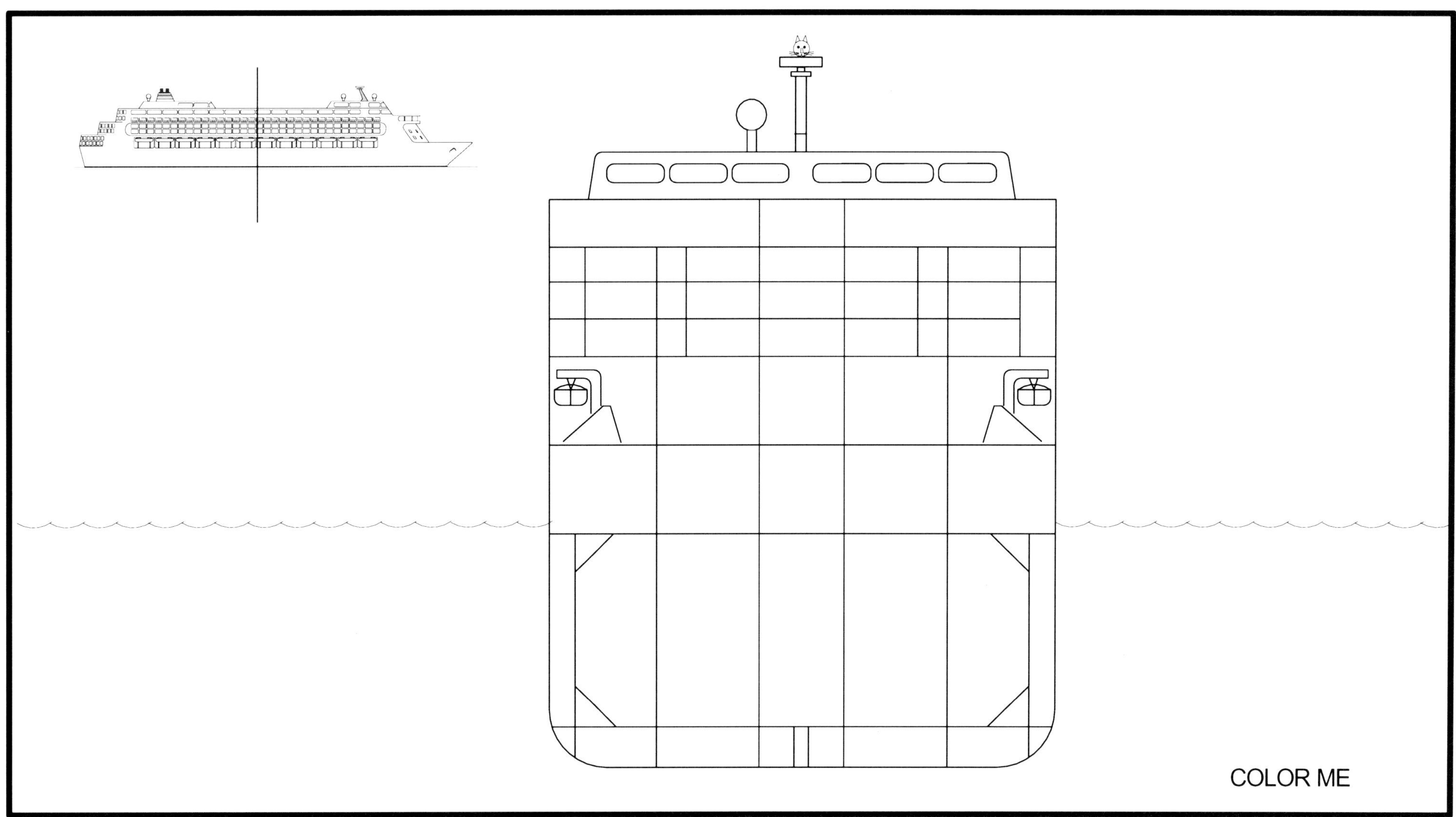

18

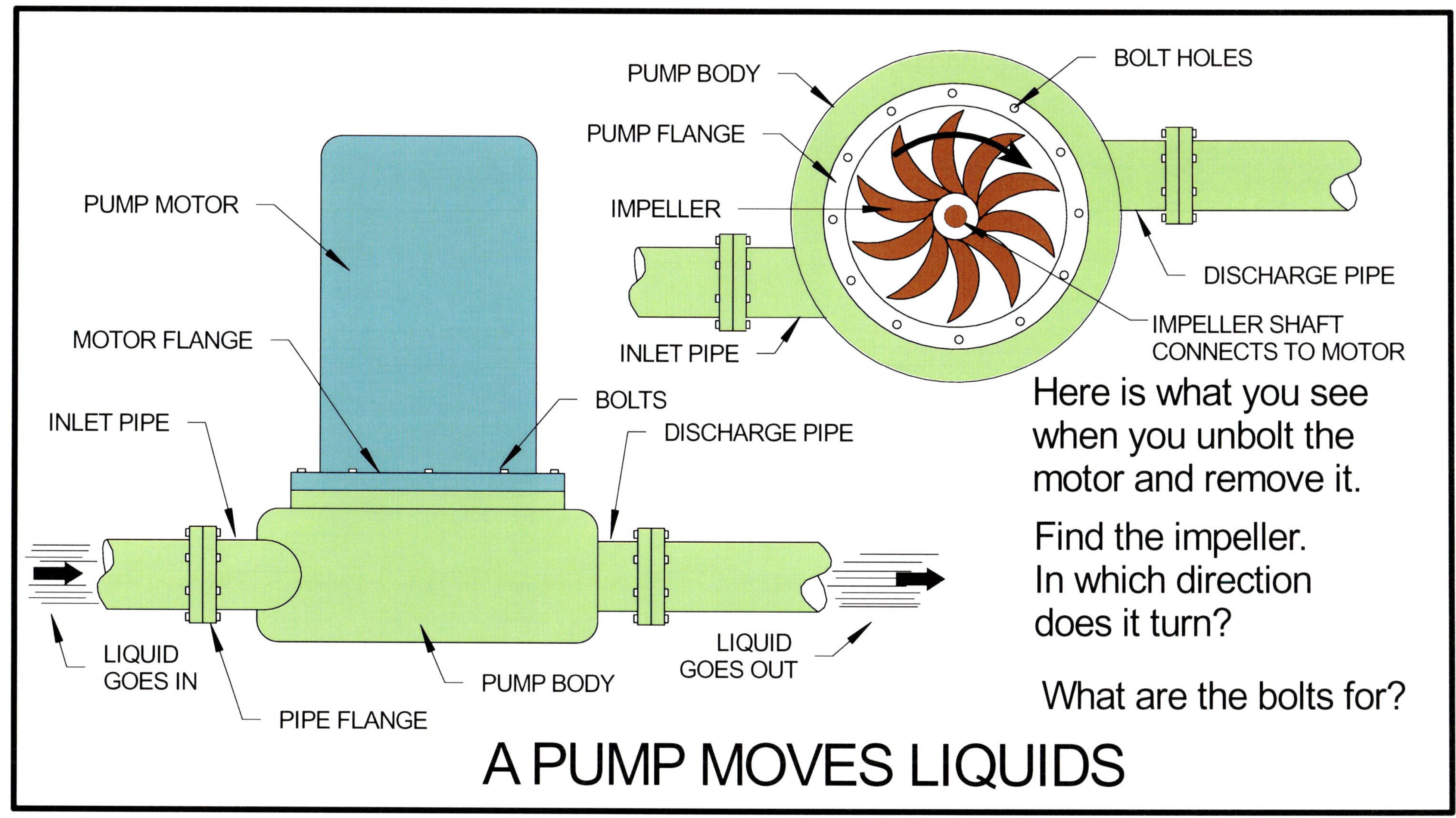

PUMP BODY
BOLT HOLES
PUMP FLANGE
IMPELLER
DISCHARGE PIPE
INLET PIPE
IMPELLER SHAFT
CONNECTS TO MOTOR
PUMP MOTOR
MOTOR FLANGE
BOLTS
DISCHARGE PIPE
INLET PIPE
LIQUID
GOES IN
PIPE FLANGE
PUMP BODY
LIQUID
GOES OUT
Here is what you see when you unbolt the motor and remove it.
Find the impeller. In which direction does it turn?
What are the bolts for?
A PUMP MOVES LIQUIDS

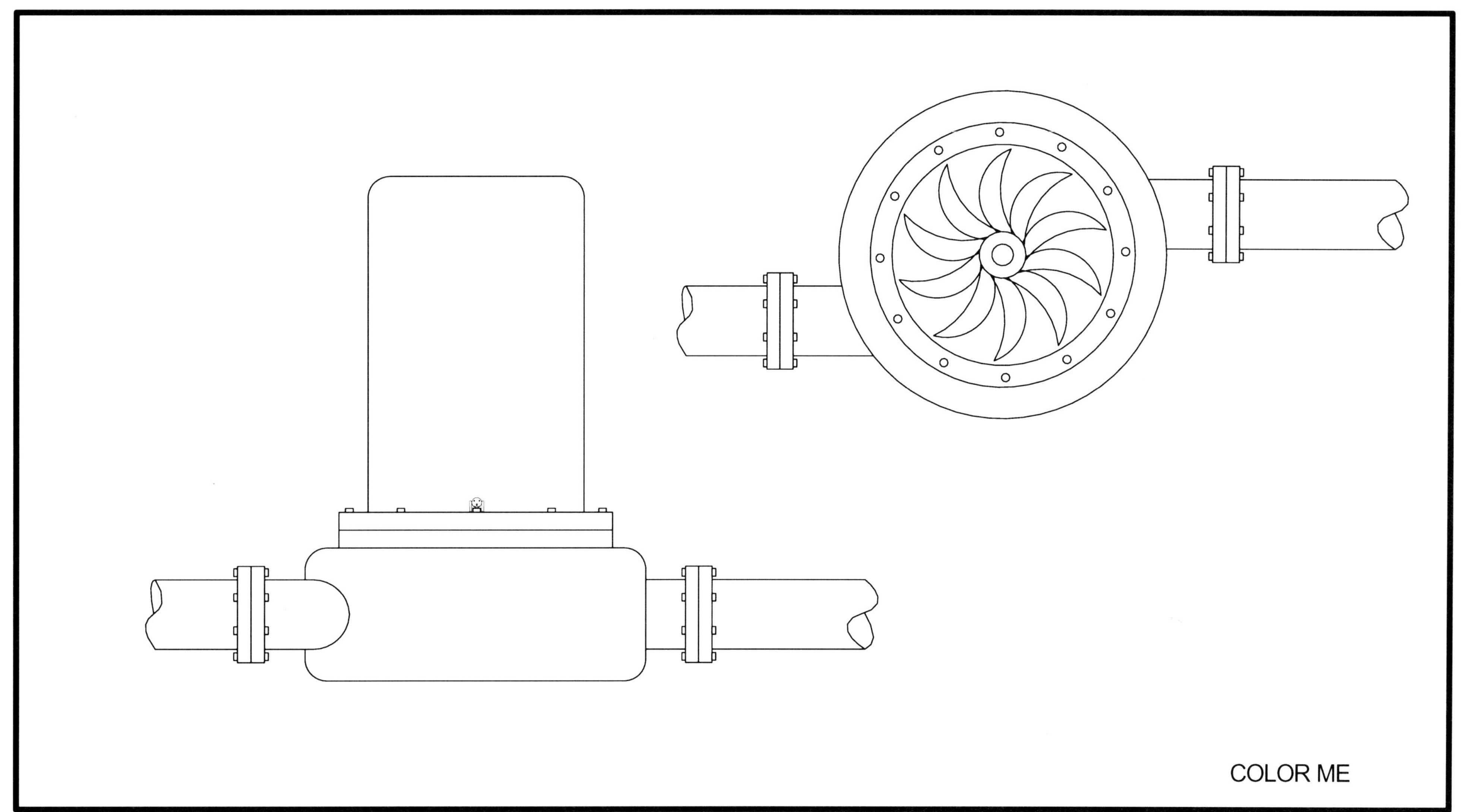

20

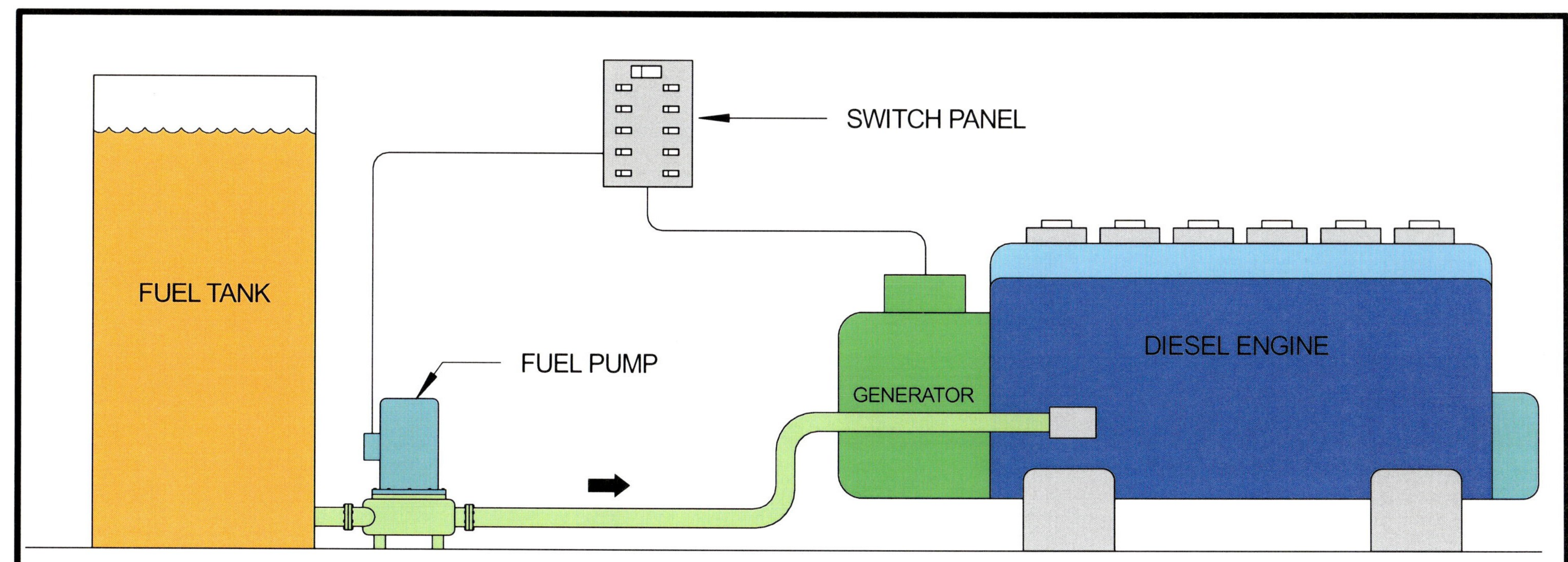

What does the arrow indicate?

The switch panel controls the pump motor.
Which switch would stop the pump from pumping?

HERE IS A PUMP MOVING FUEL TO A DIESEL ENGINE

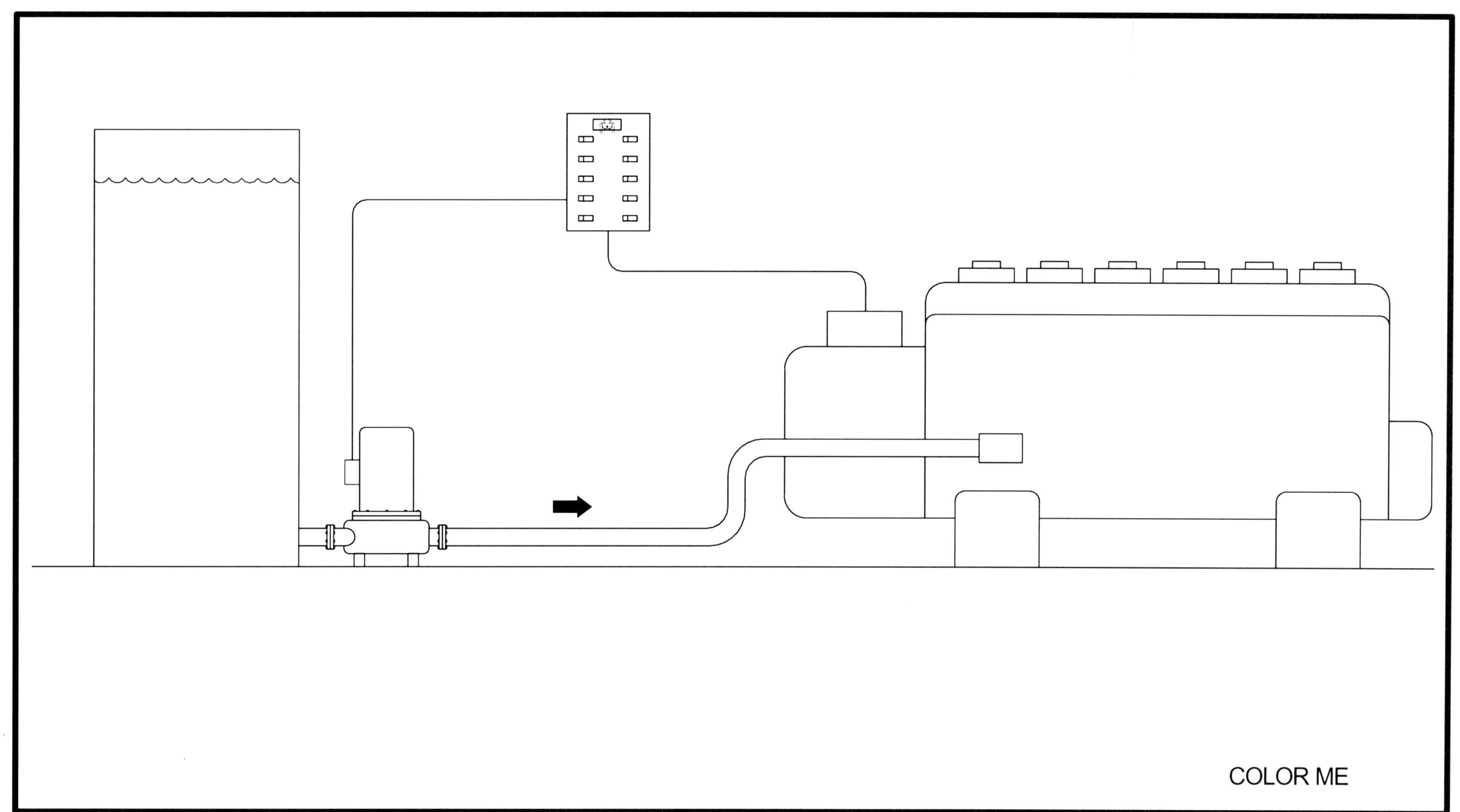
COLOR ME

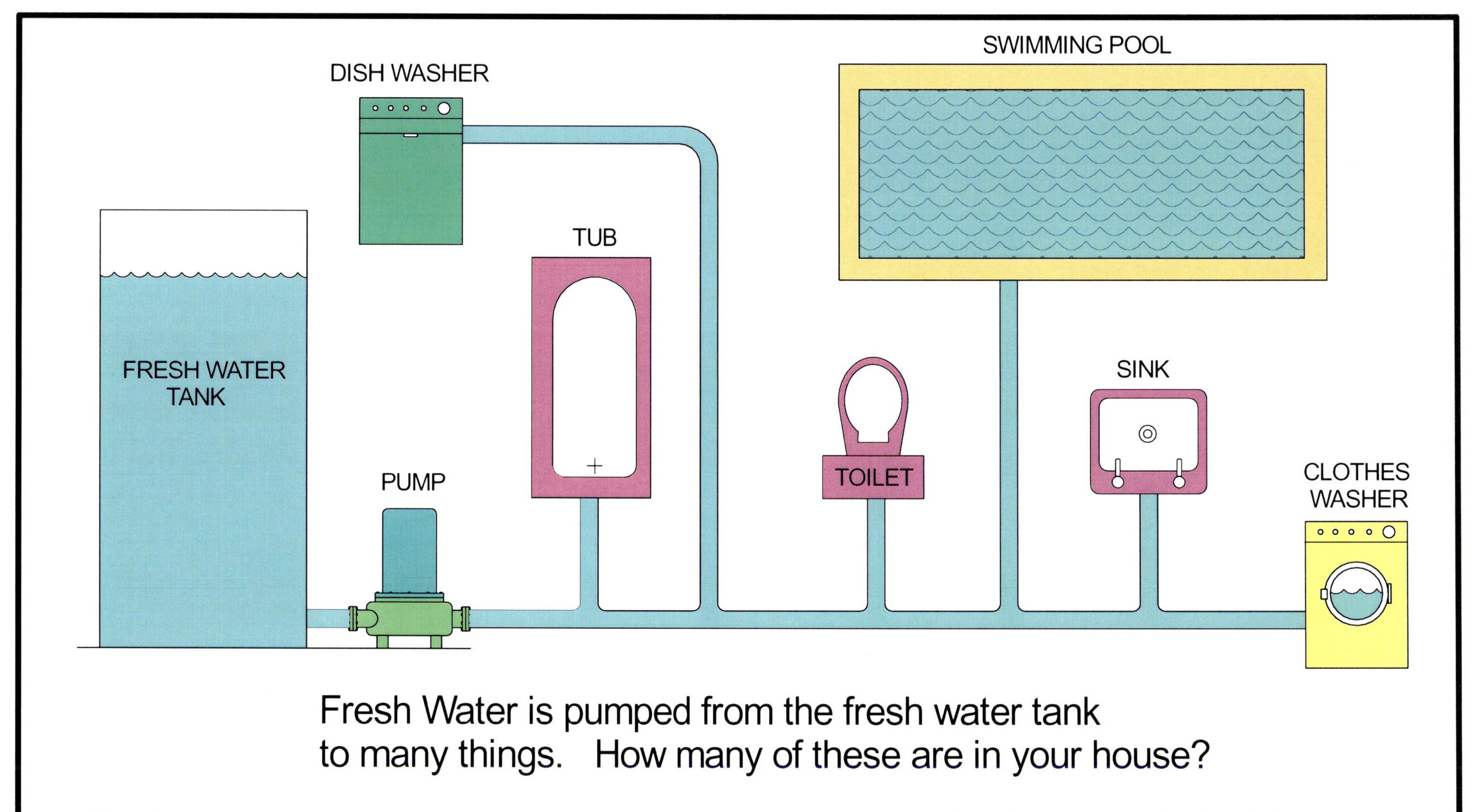

Fresh Water is pumped from the fresh water tank to many things.   How many of these are in your house?

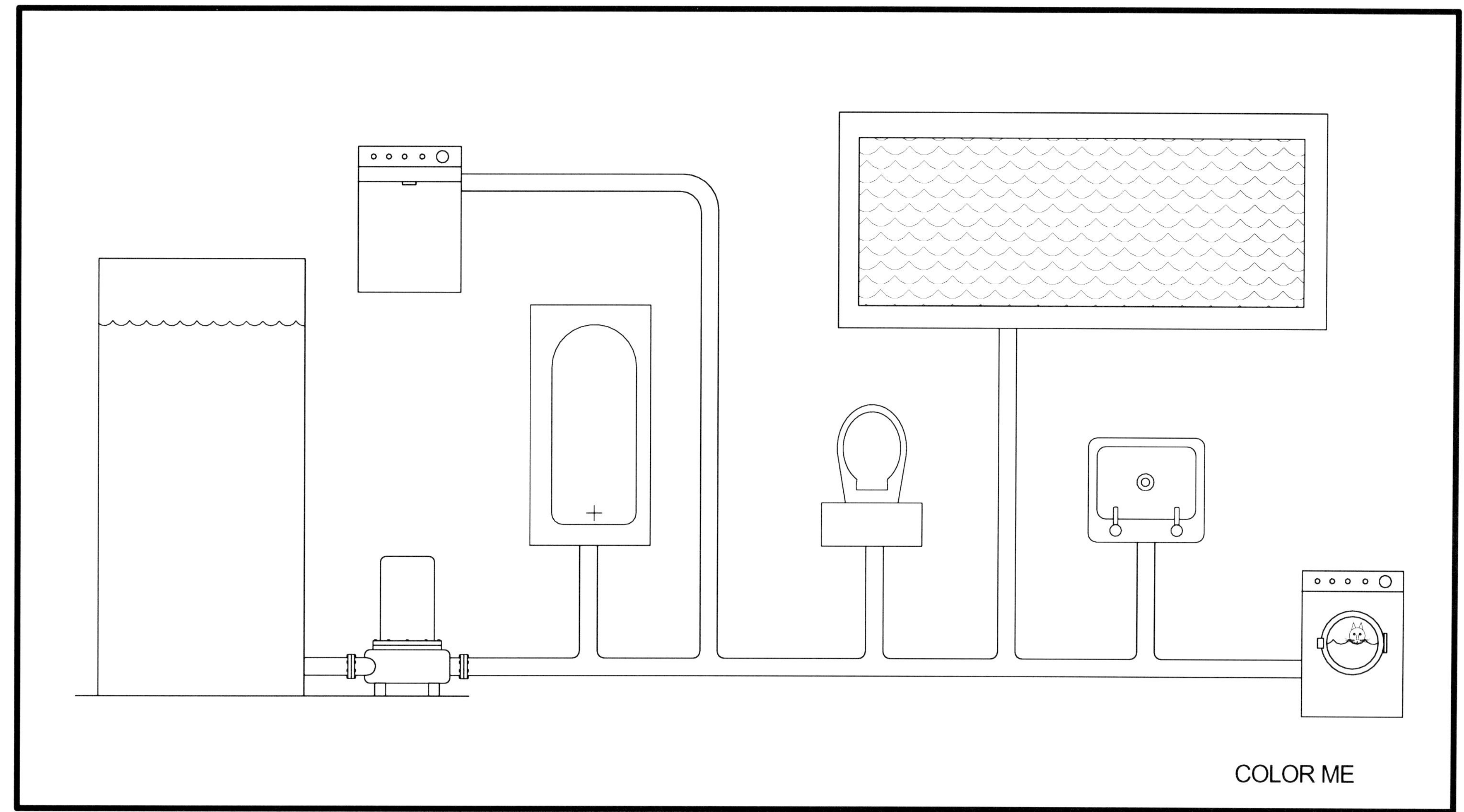
COLOR ME

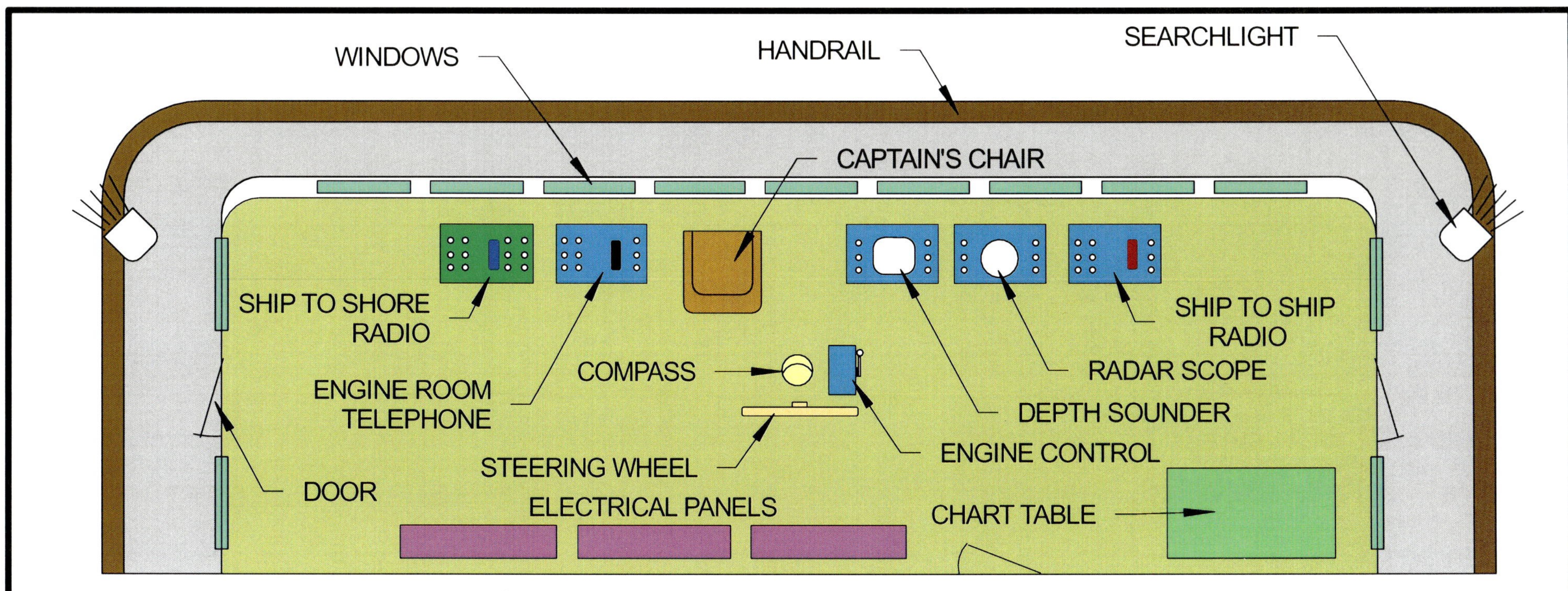

THE CAPTAIN CONTROLS THE SHIP FROM THE BRIDGE

The Bridge has lots of equipment. The following pages will tell you what each piece does, and how each one helps the Captain.

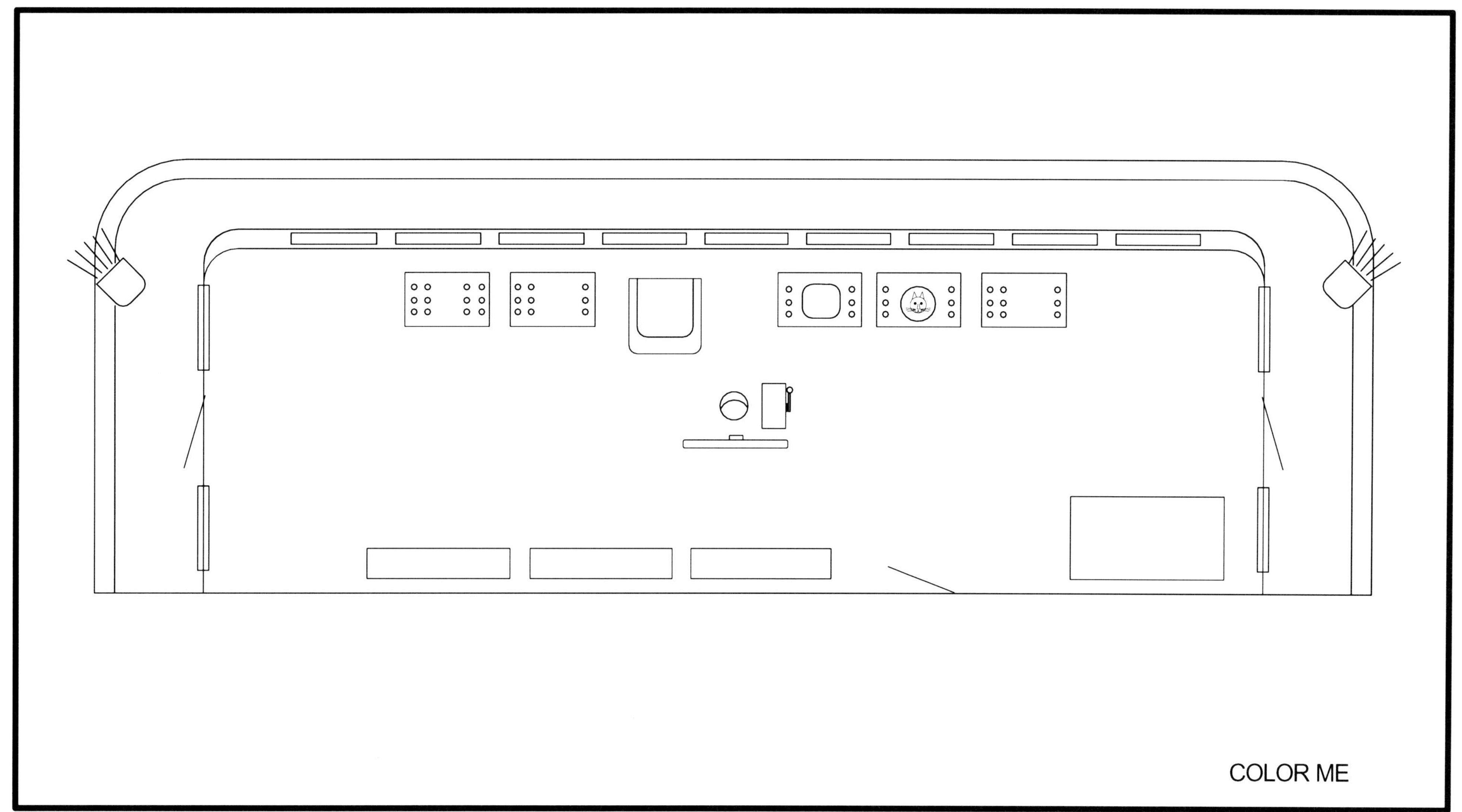
COLOR ME

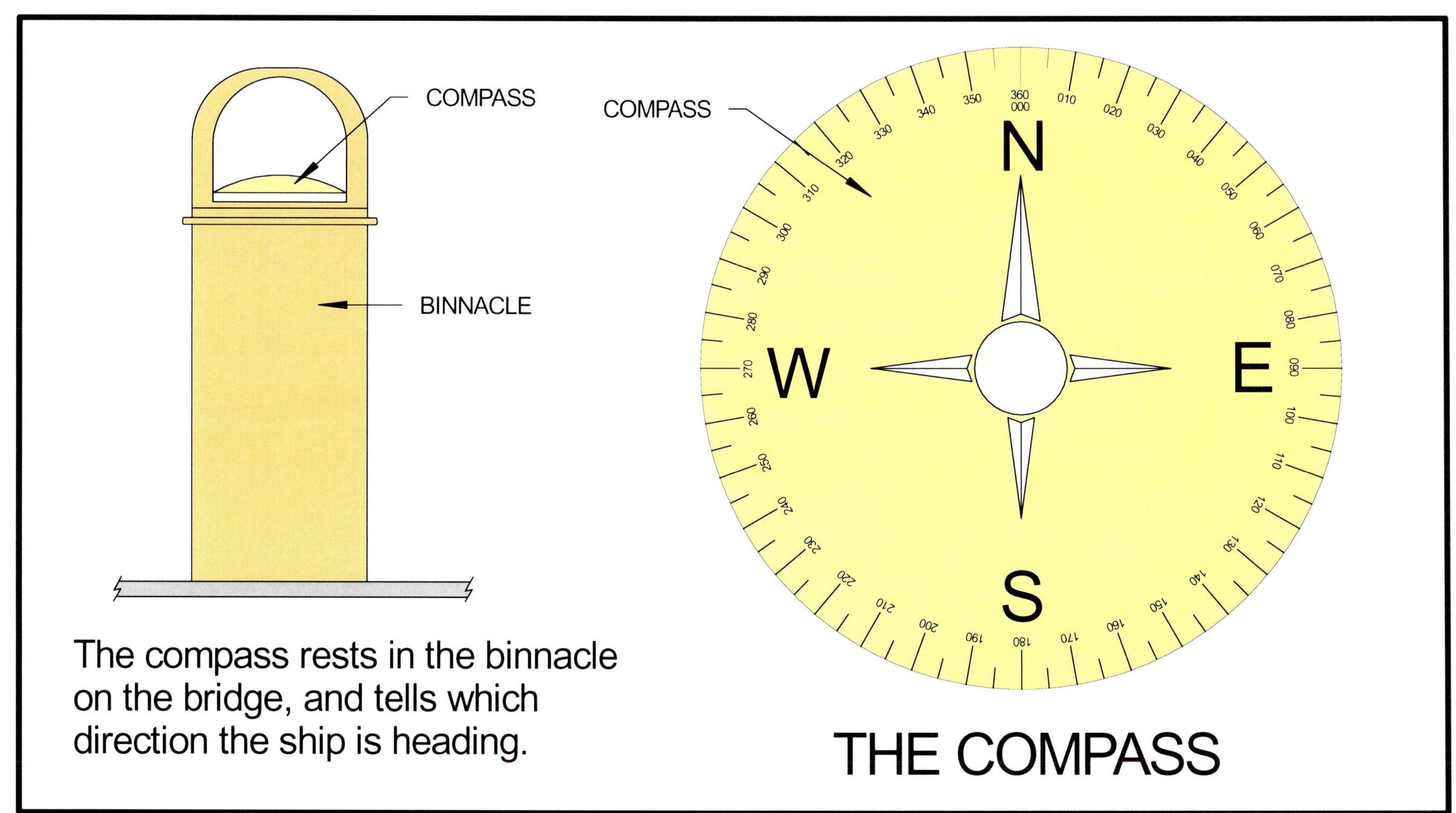

The compass rests in the binnacle on the bridge, and tells which direction the ship is heading.

THE COMPASS

N
W
E
S
360
000
010
020
030
040
050
060
070
080
090
100
110
120
130
140
150
160
170
180
190
200
210
220
230
240
250
260
270
280
290
300
310
320
330
340
350

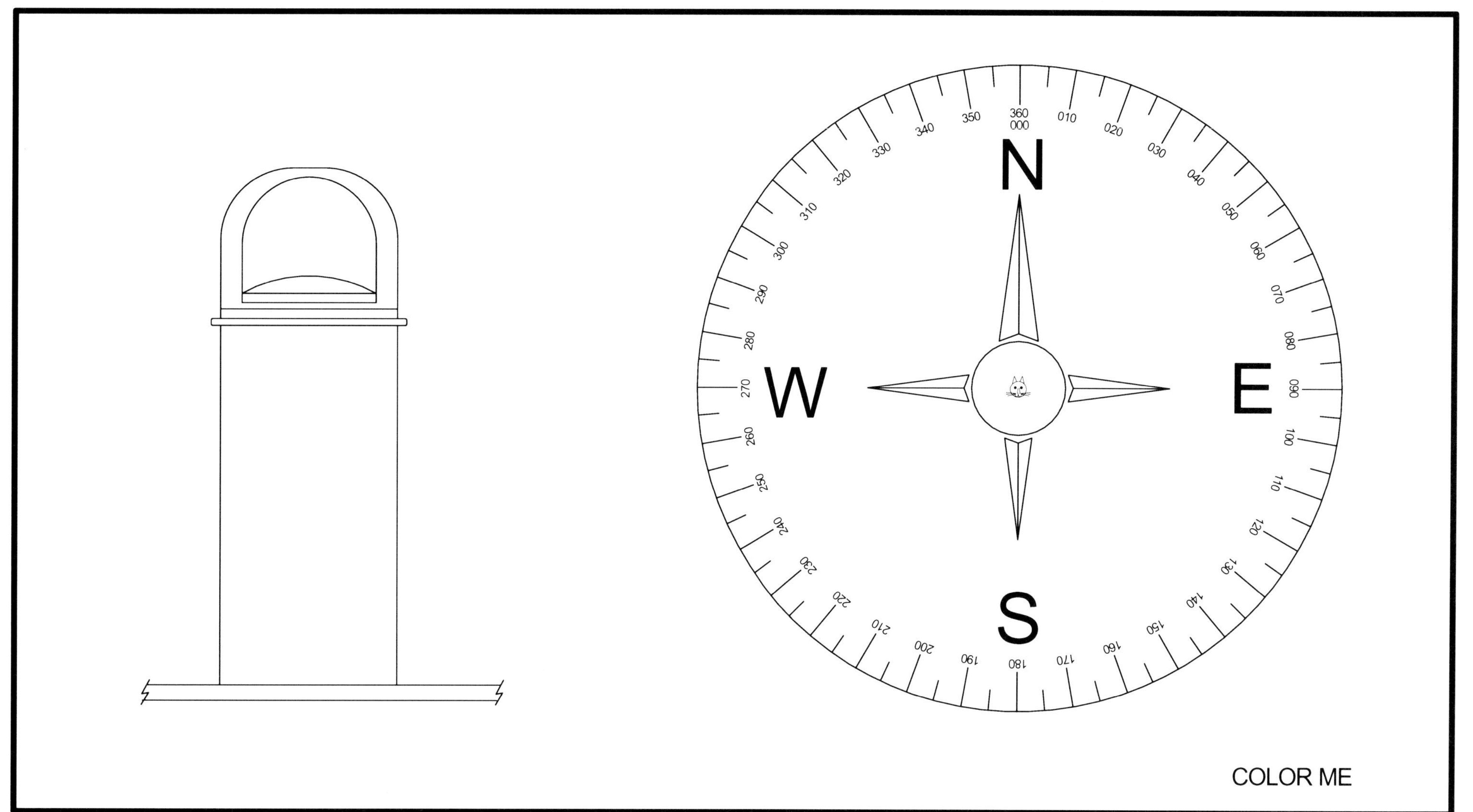

COLOR ME

28

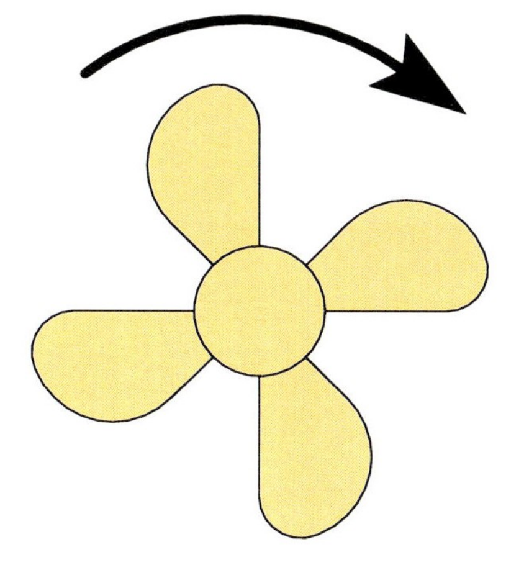

The engine control on the bridge makes the propeller turn clockwise or counter-clockwise.   It also controls the how fast the propeller turns.

When the propeller turns clockwise, the ship moves ahead or forward.

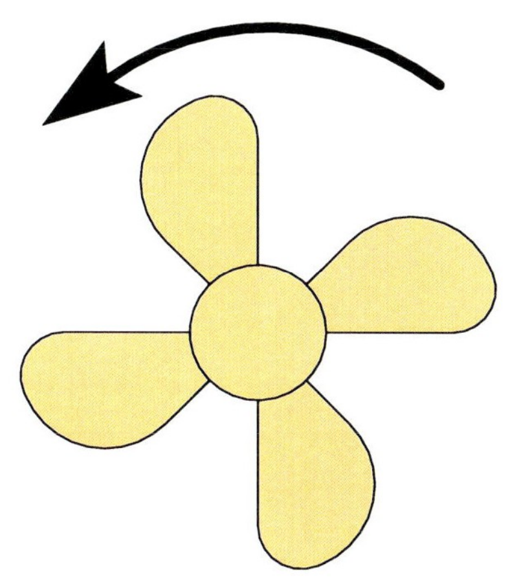

When the propeller turns counter-clockwise, the ship moves astern or backward.

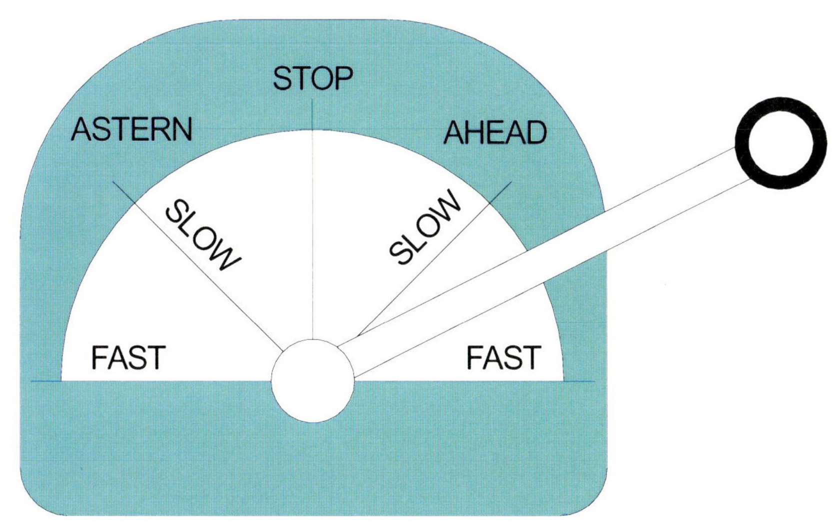

THE ENGINE CONTROL

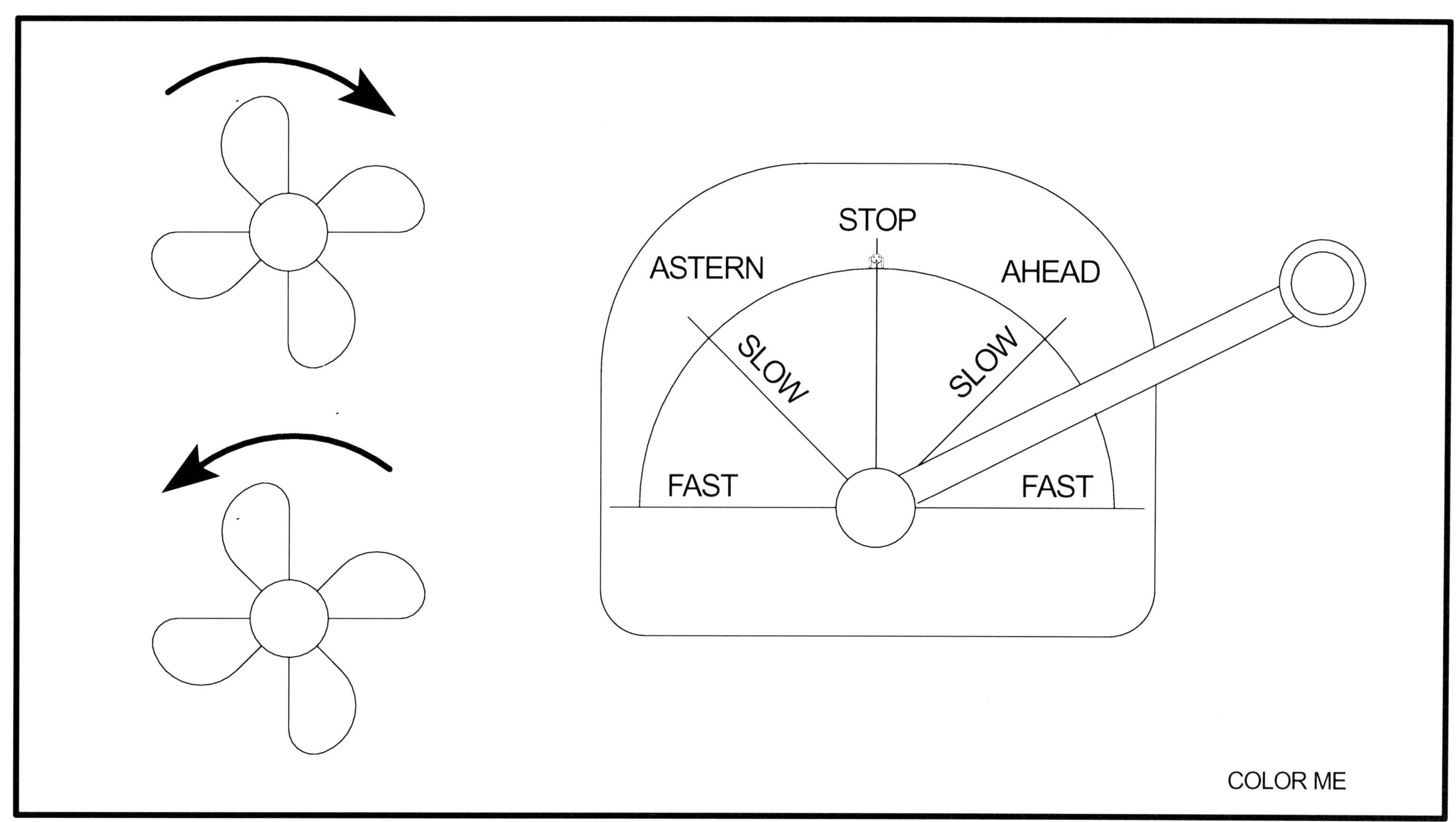

30

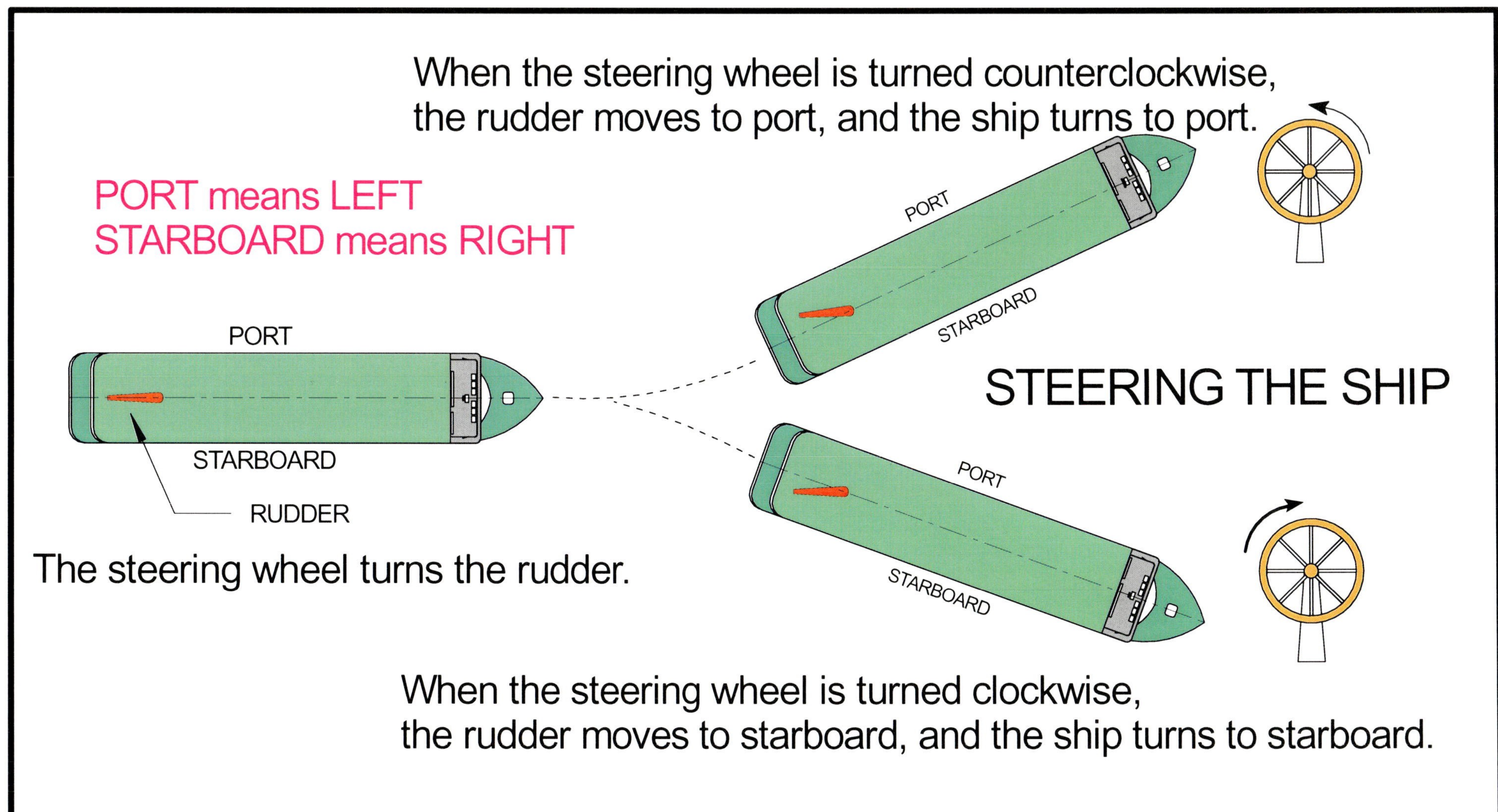
When the steering wheel is turned counterclockwise, the rudder moves to port, and the ship turns to port.
PORT means LEFT
STARBOARD means RIGHT
PORT
STARBOARD
PORT
STARBOARD
RUDDER
The steering wheel turns the rudder.
STEERING THE SHIP
PORT
STARBOARD
When the steering wheel is turned clockwise, the rudder moves to starboard, and the ship turns to starboard.

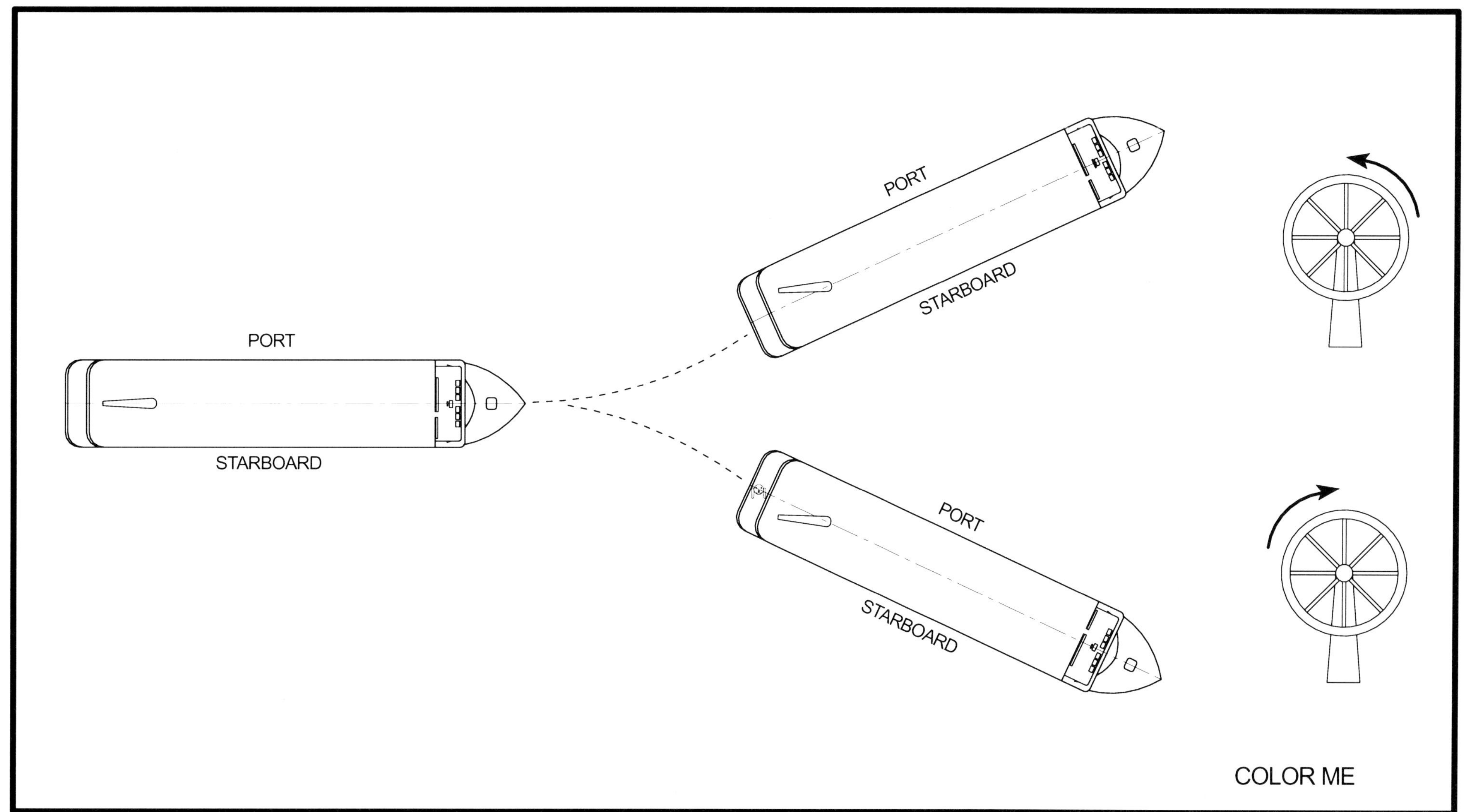

PORT
STARBOARD
PORT
STARBOARD
PORT
STARBOARD
COLOR ME

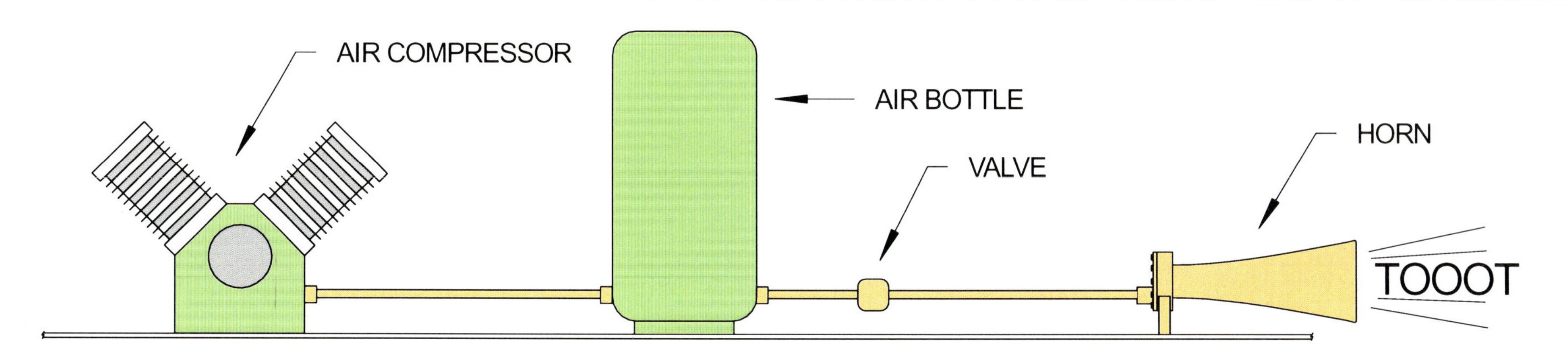

The Ship's Horn, on the top deck, is used to signal other ships when they meet, and during periods of foggy weather.

Sometimes the Ship's Horn is used by the Captain to tell the passengers that the ship is ready to leave the dock.

The air compressor pushes air into the air bottle where it is stored. When the Captain pushes a button on the bridge, the valve opens and sends air from the air bottle to the horn, making it sound.

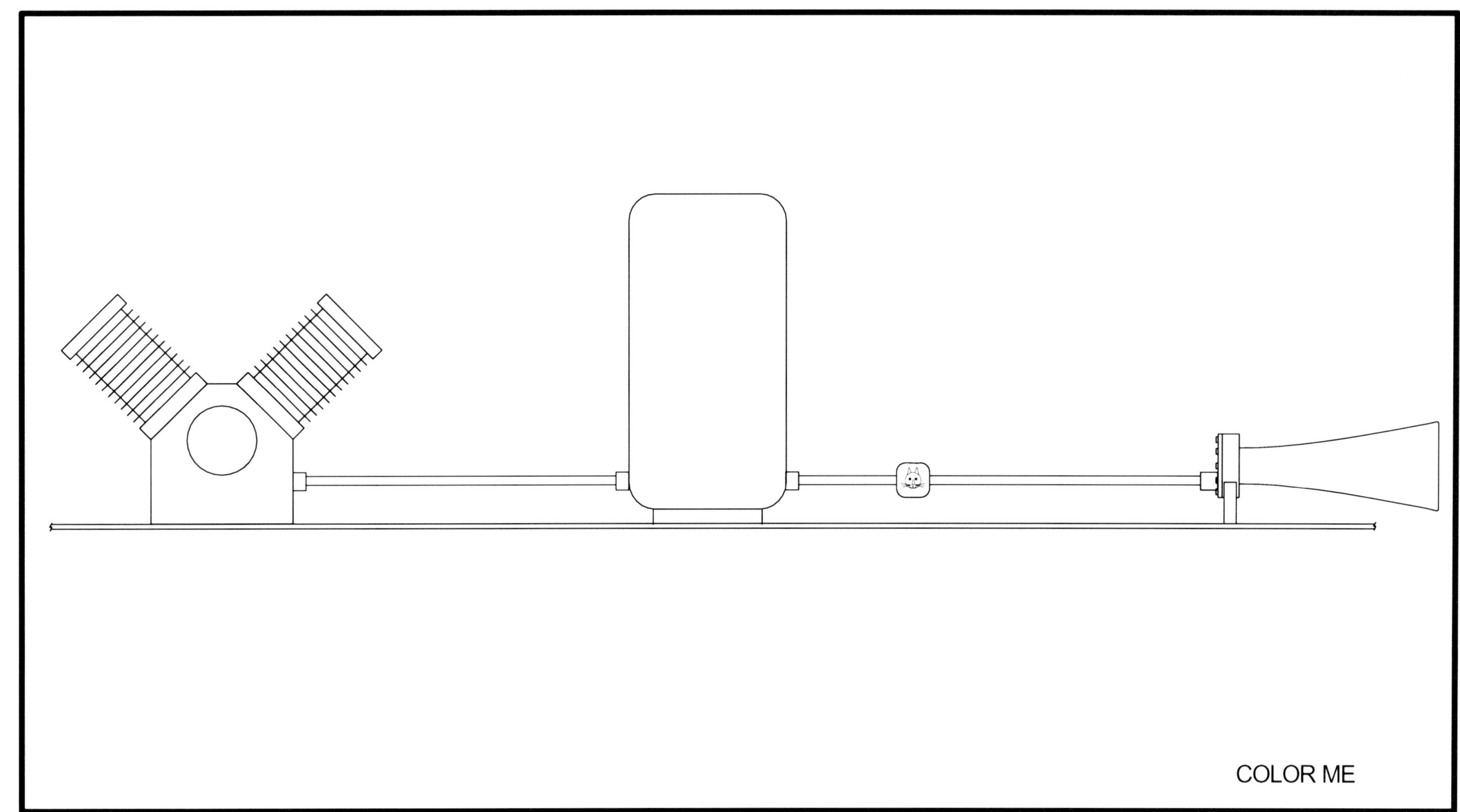
COLOR ME

RADAR means <u>RA</u>dio <u>D</u>etection <u>A</u>nd <u>R</u>anging.

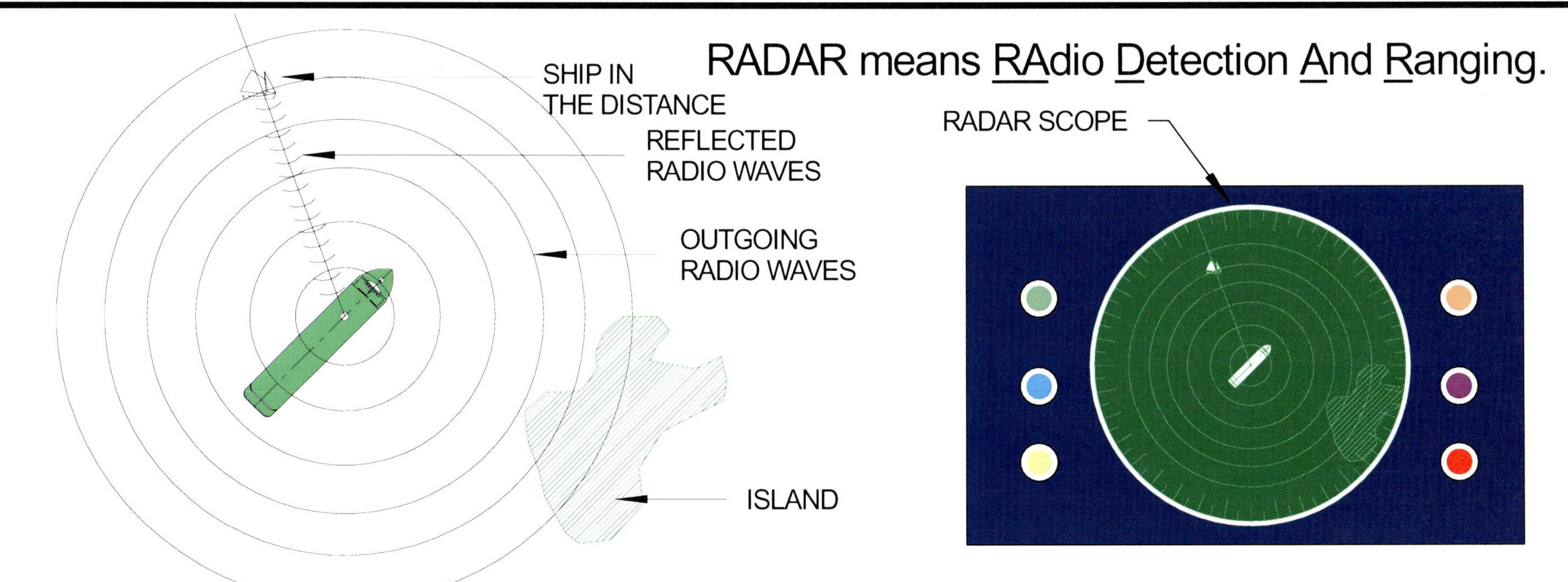

The radar scope on the bridge sends out radio waves
from the radar antenna on the top deck. These radio waves
bounce off other ships and land masses and tell the Captain
the direction and distance they are from his ship.

RADAR

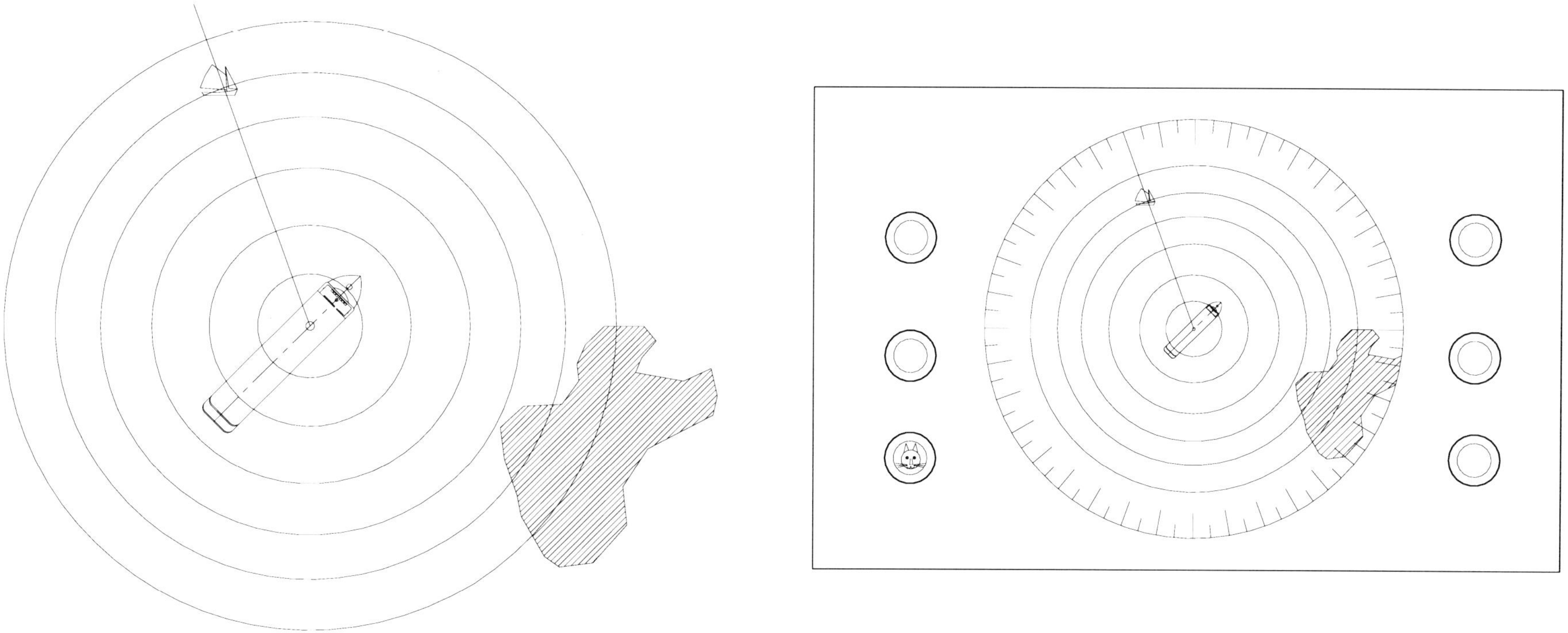

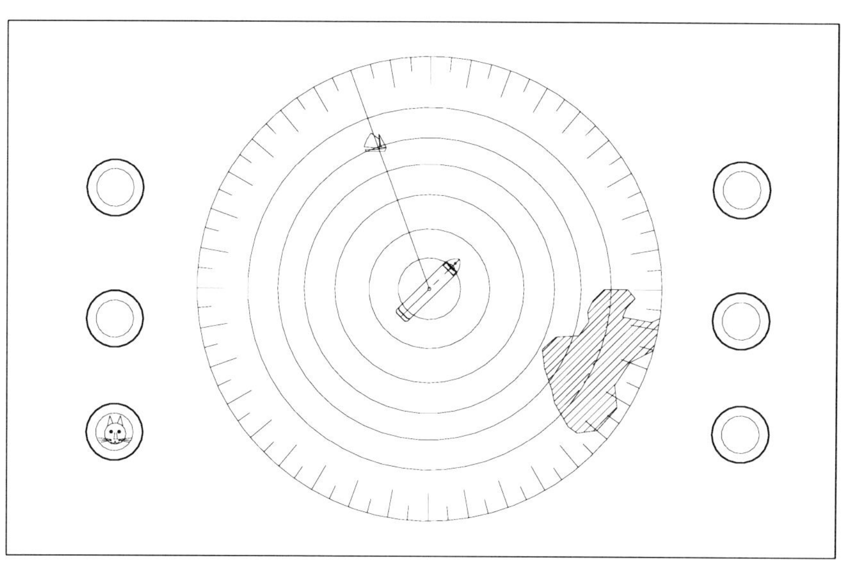

COLOR ME

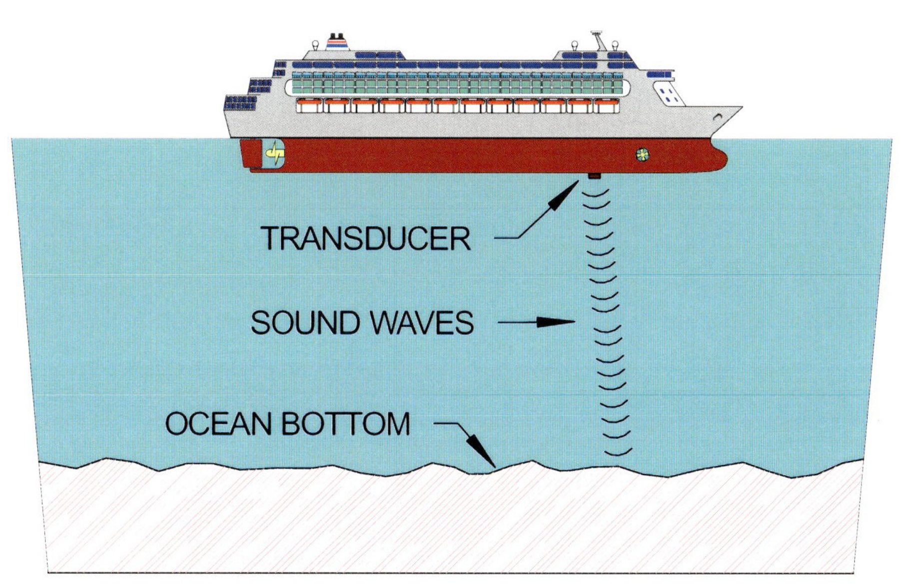

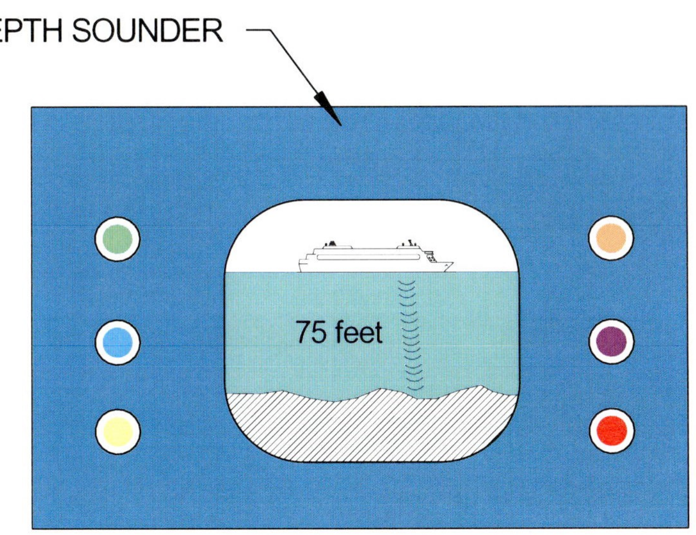

The Depth Sounder on the bridge sends out sound waves from the Transducer on the ship's bottom. These sound waves bounce off the ocean bottom and tell the Captain how deep the ocean is under his ship.

DEPTH SOUNDER

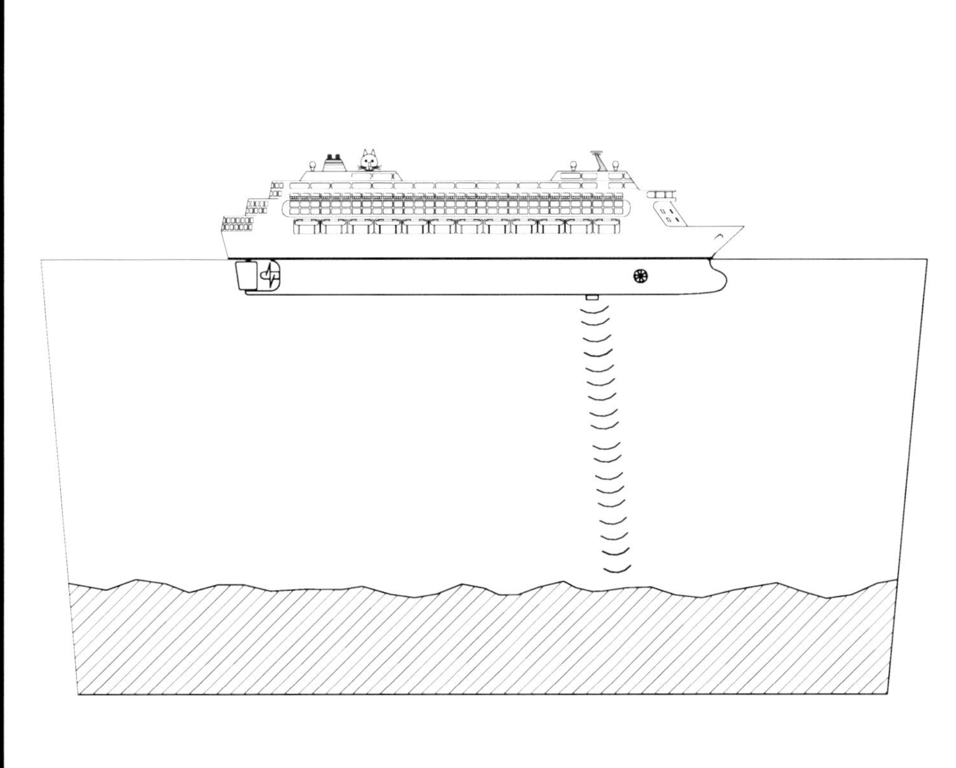
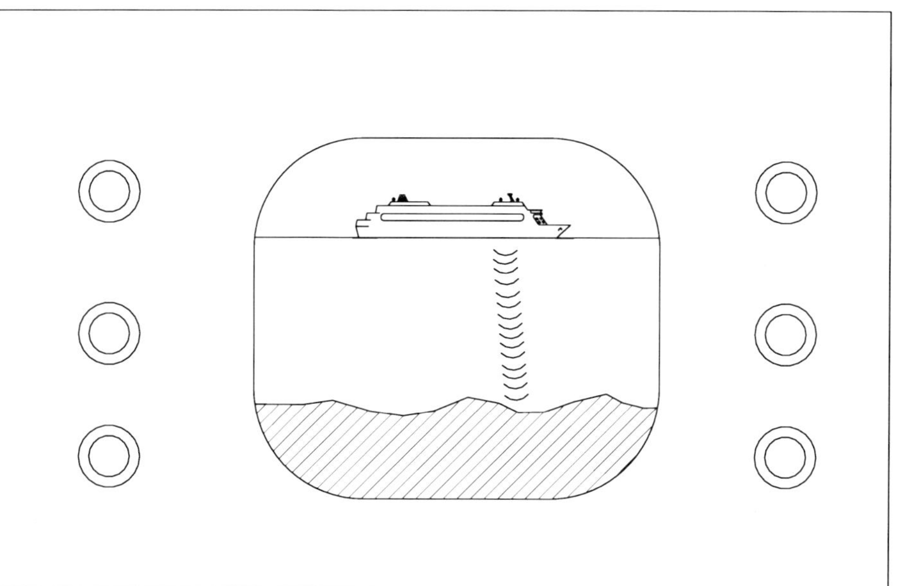

COLOR ME

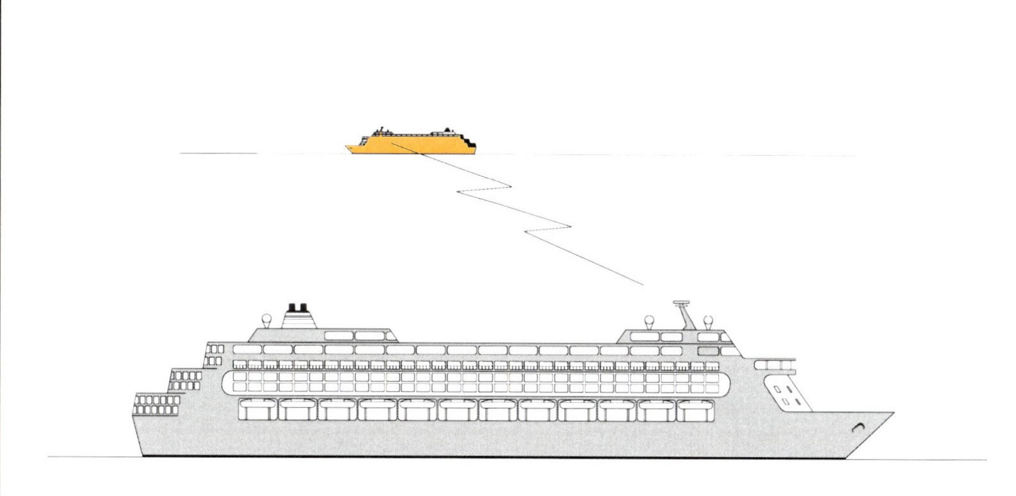
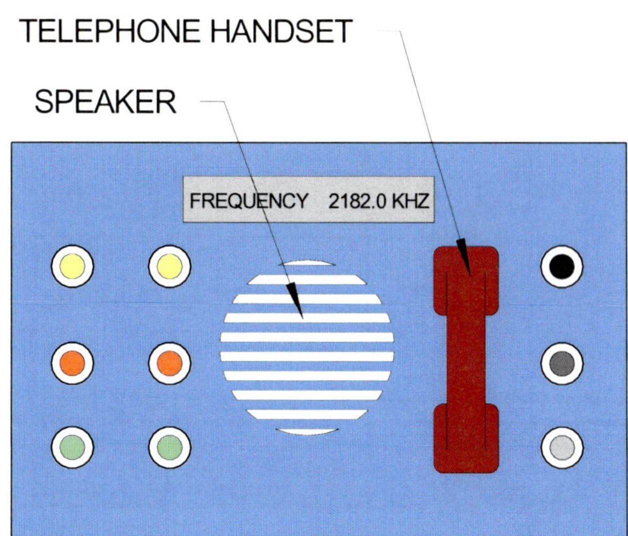

The ship to ship radio telephone allows the Captain to talk to the captains of other ships at sea.

The telephone handset allows him to have private conversations, while the speaker allows everyone on the bridge to hear the other ship.

SHIP TO SHIP RADIO TELEPHONE

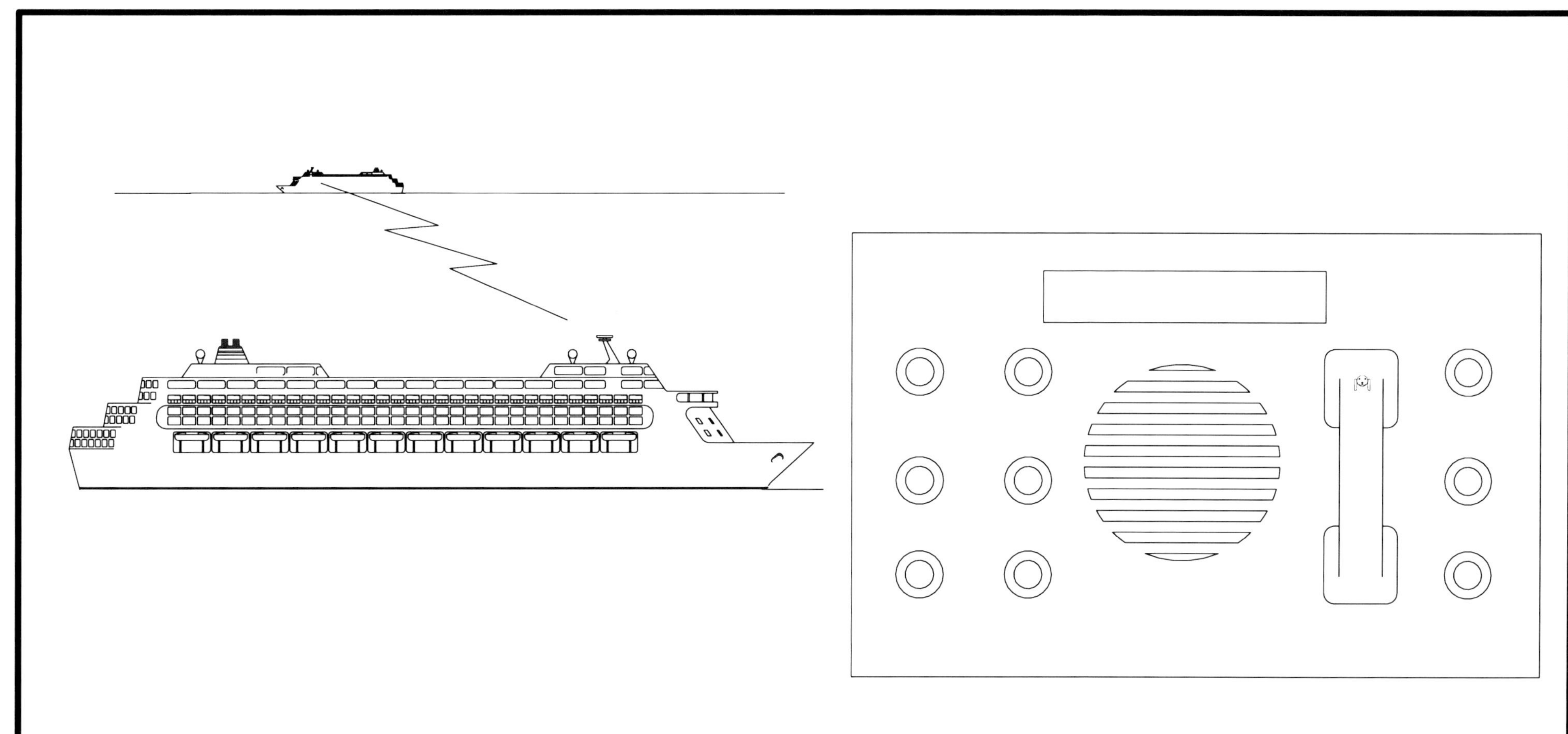

COLOR ME

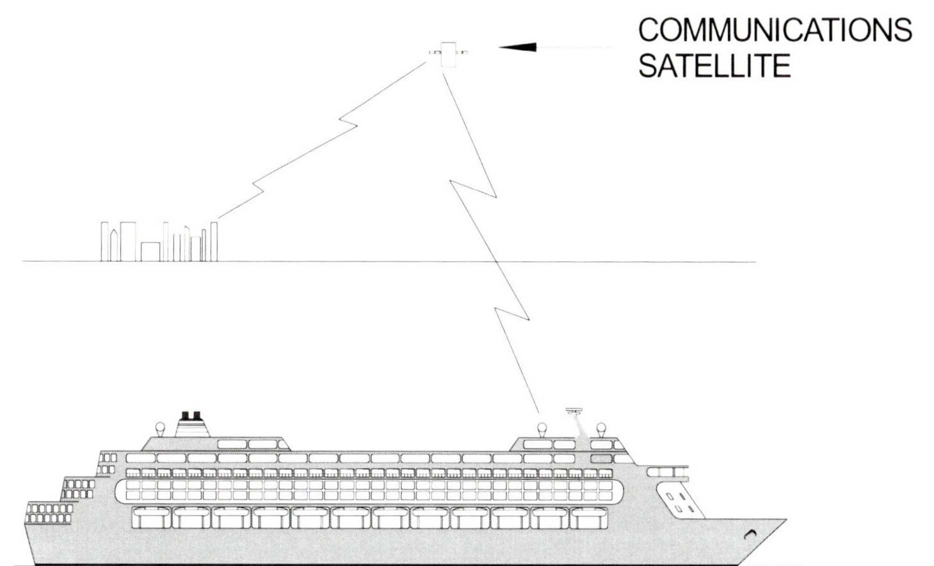

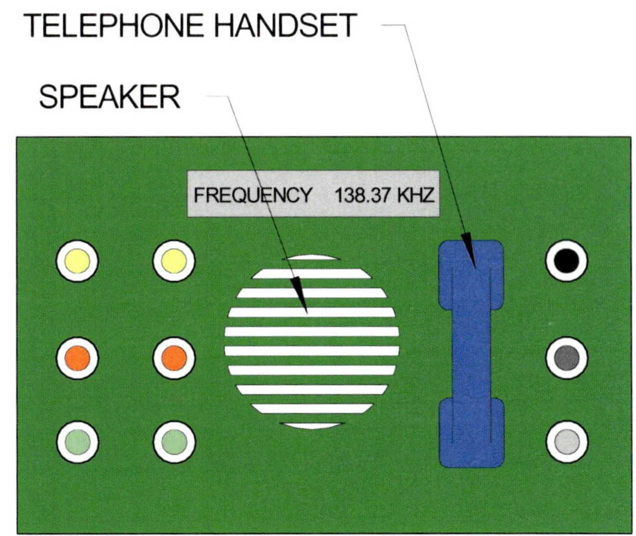

The ship to shore radio telephone is similar to the ship to ship radio,
but it allows the Captain to talk to the home office and other shore telephones.
This radio bounces its signal off a communications satellite.

The telephone handset allows private conversations, while the speaker
allows everyone on the bridge to hear the conversation.

SHIP TO SHORE RADIO TELEPHONE

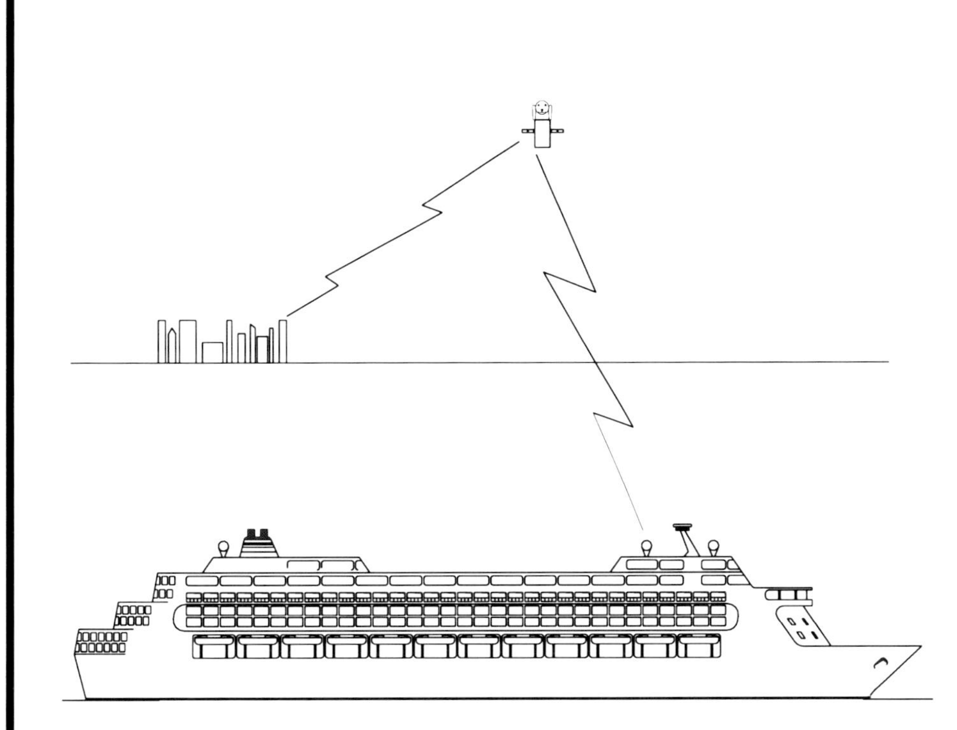

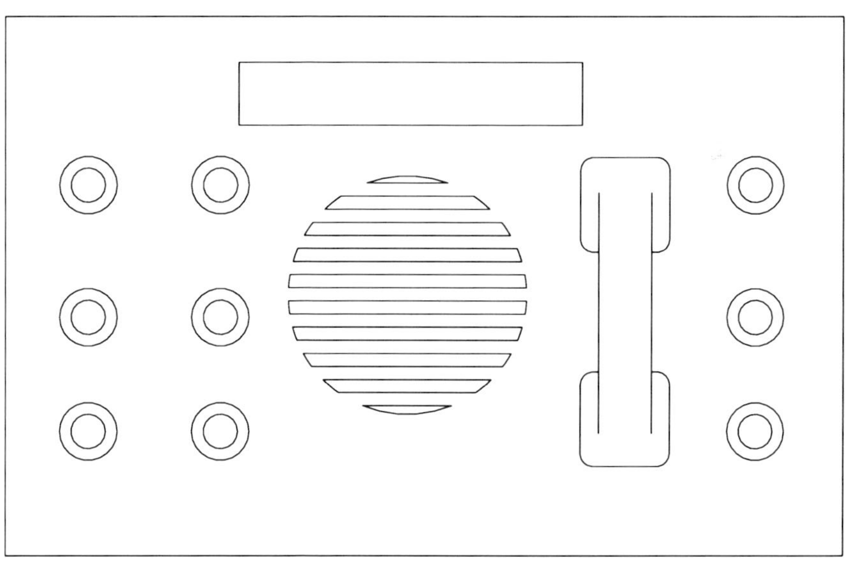

COLOR ME

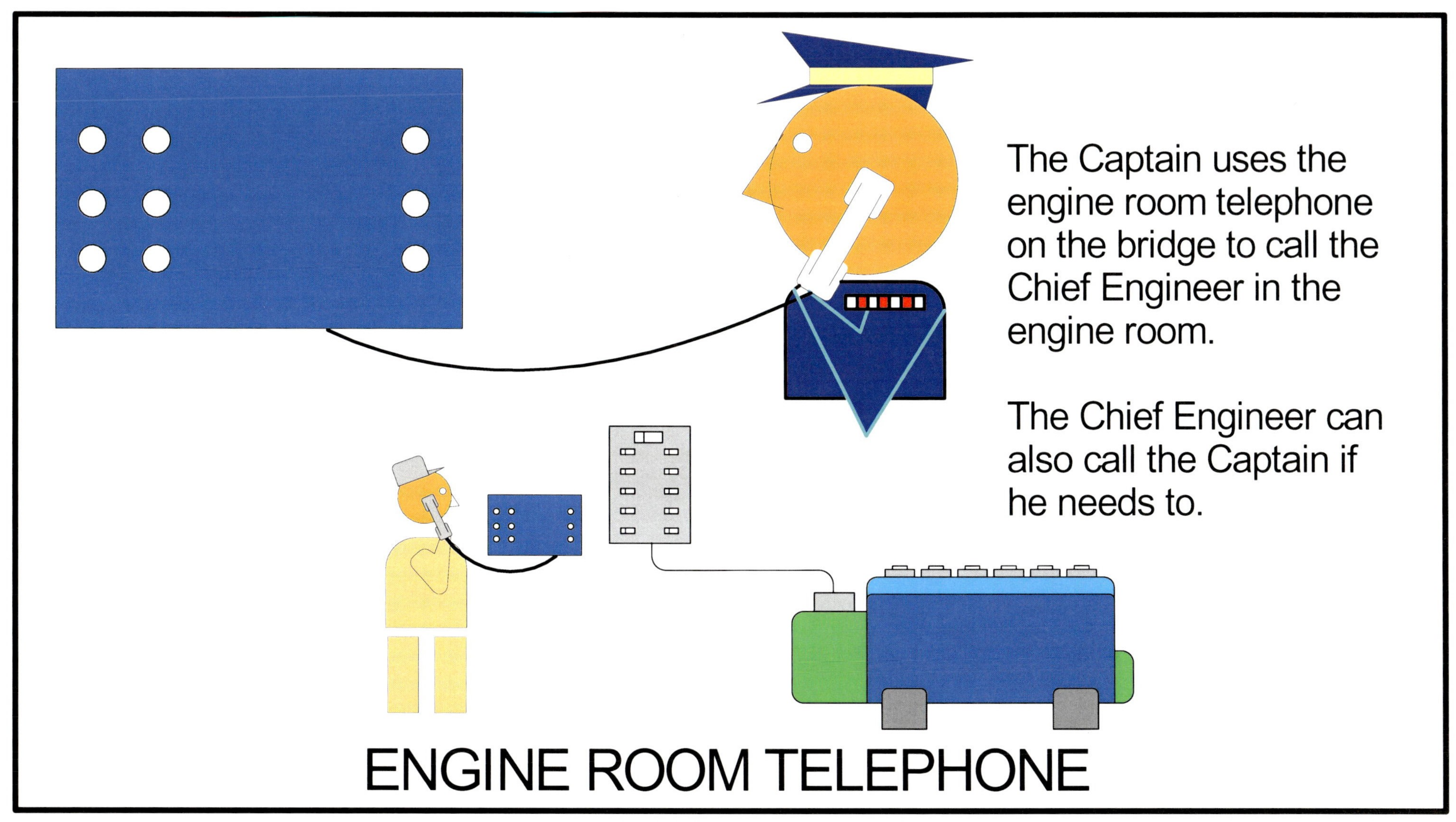

The Captain uses the engine room telephone on the bridge to call the Chief Engineer in the engine room.

The Chief Engineer can also call the Captain if he needs to.

ENGINE ROOM TELEPHONE

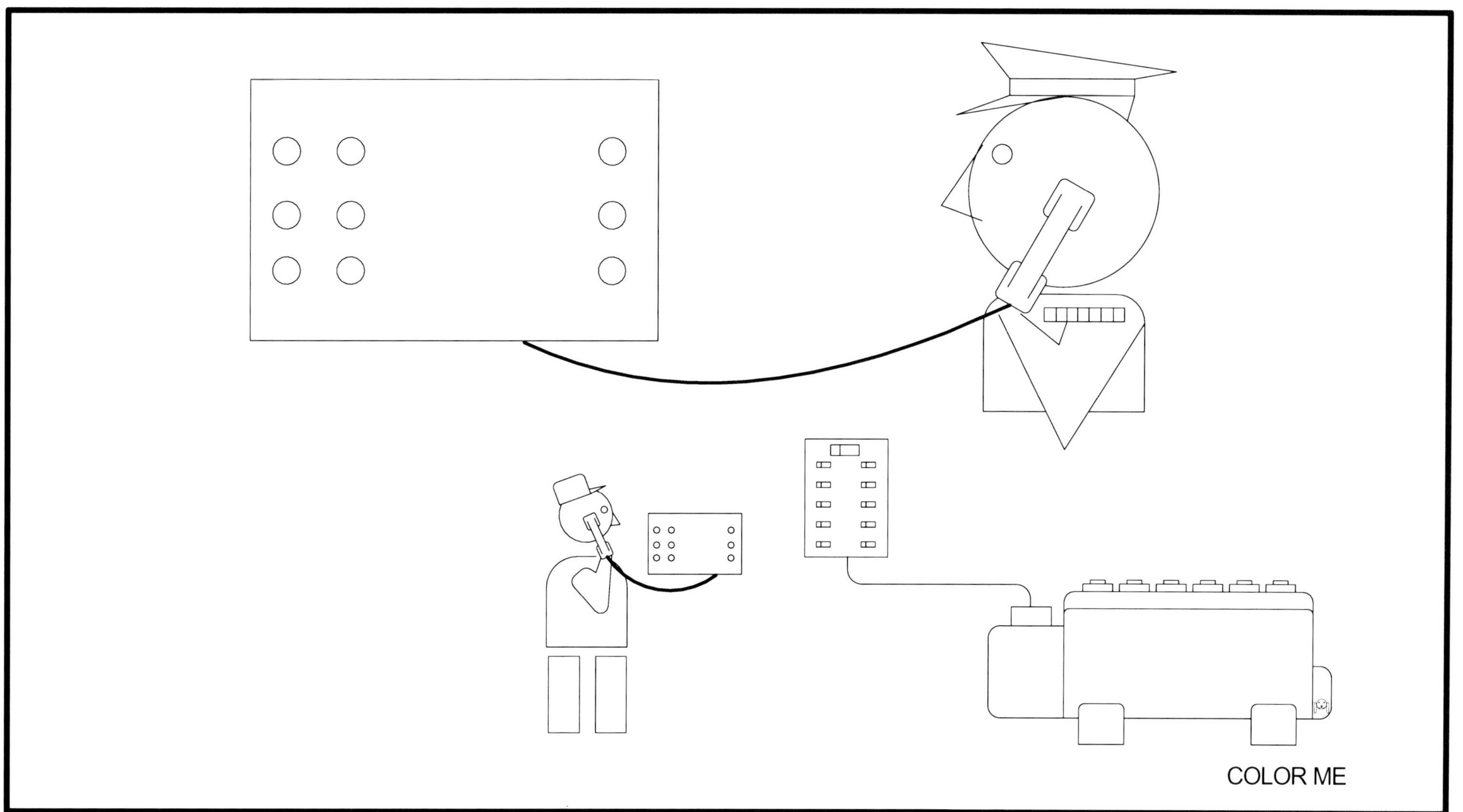

COLOR ME

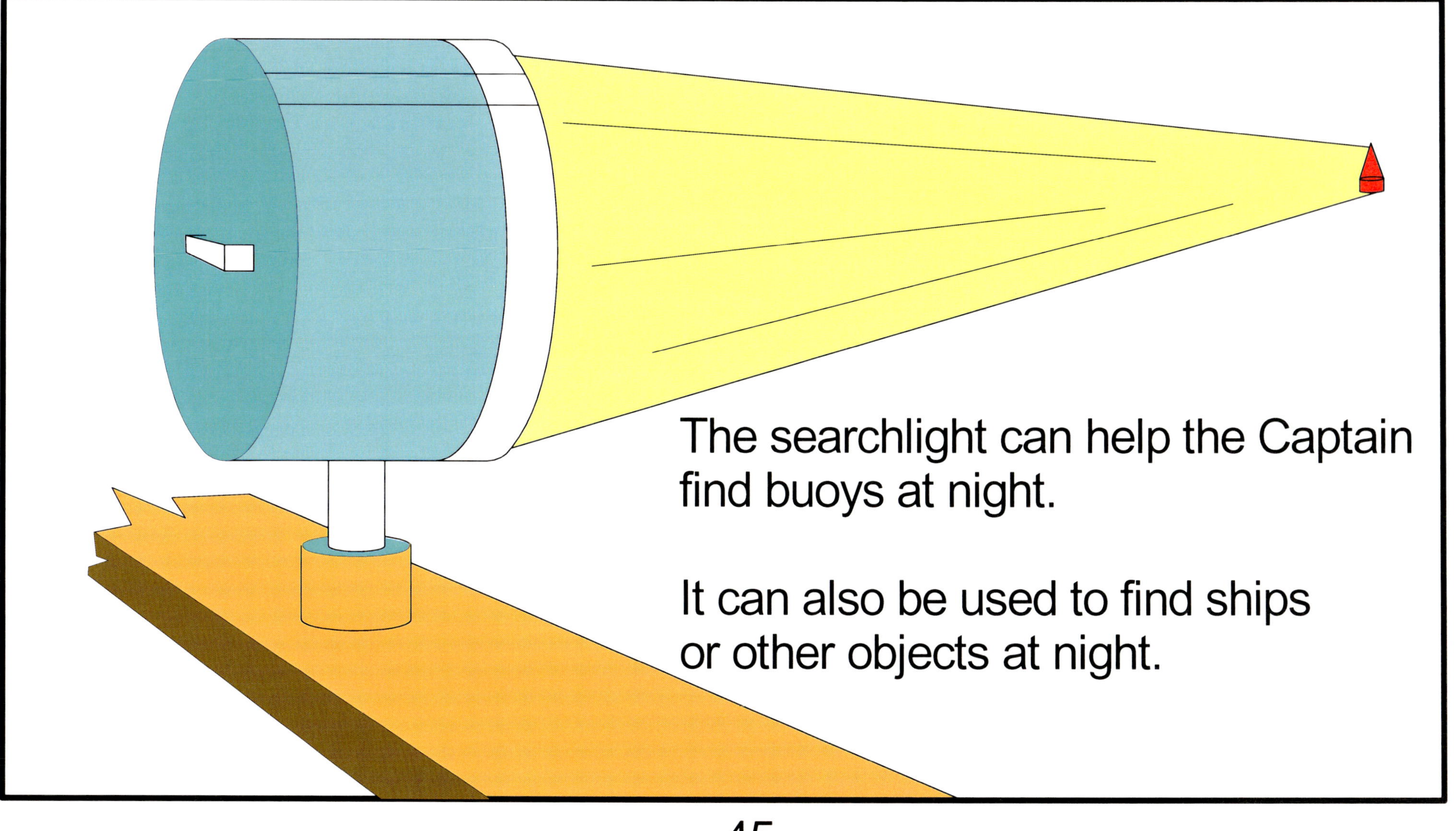
The searchlight can help the Captain
find buoys at night.

It can also be used to find ships
or other objects at night.

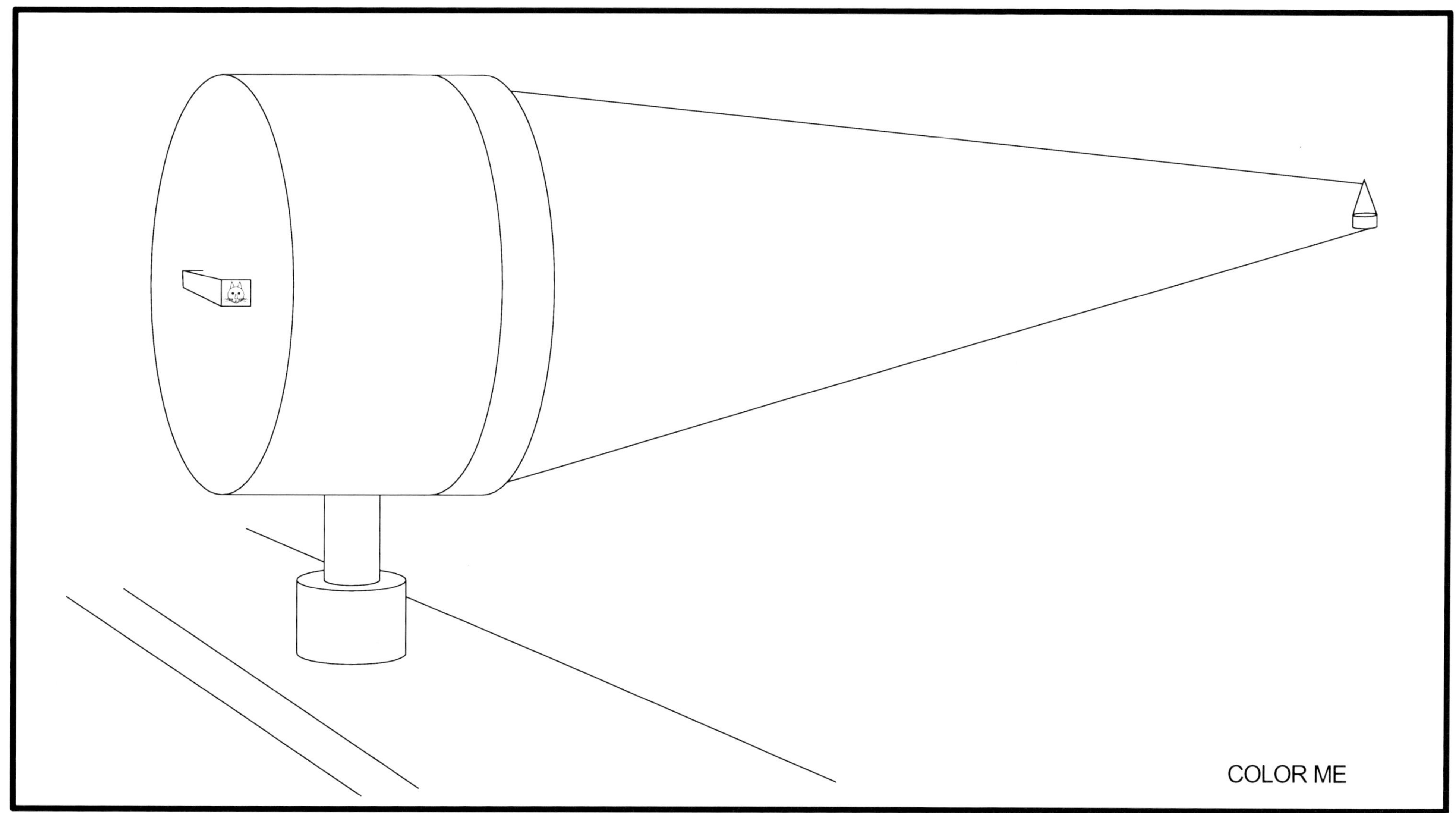

46

Each electrical panel has a purpose. The alarm signal lights indicate where and when an alarm goes off on the ship.

ELECTRICAL PANELS

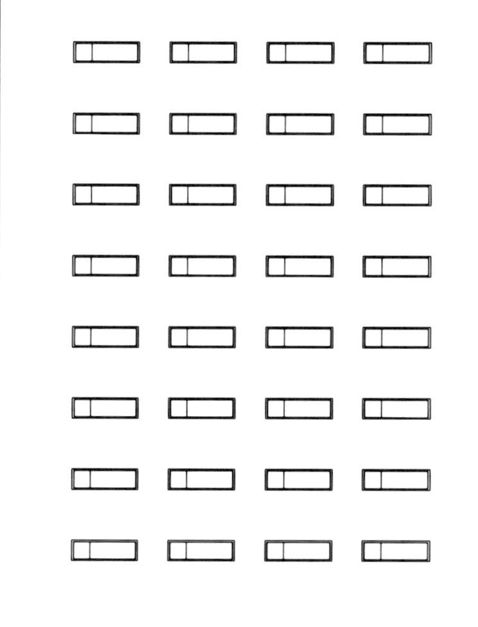
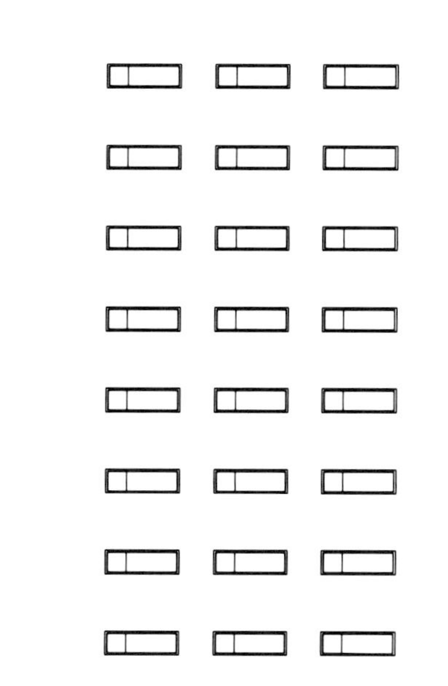

COLOR ME

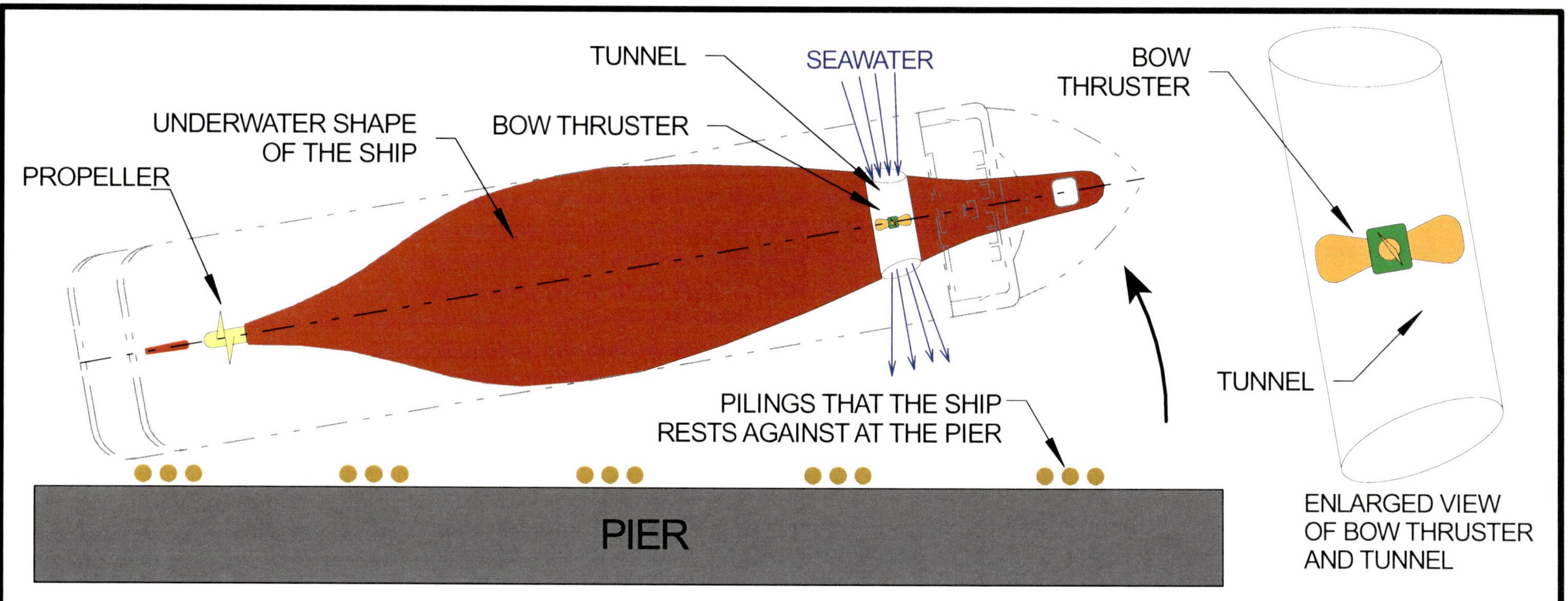

The Bow Thruster is like a sideways propeller, and it draws seawater into one end of the tunnel and pushes it out of the other end. This makes the bow of the ship move <u>away</u> from the pier.   By reversing the rotation of the thruster, the bow can be moved <u>toward</u> the pier.

BOW THRUSTER

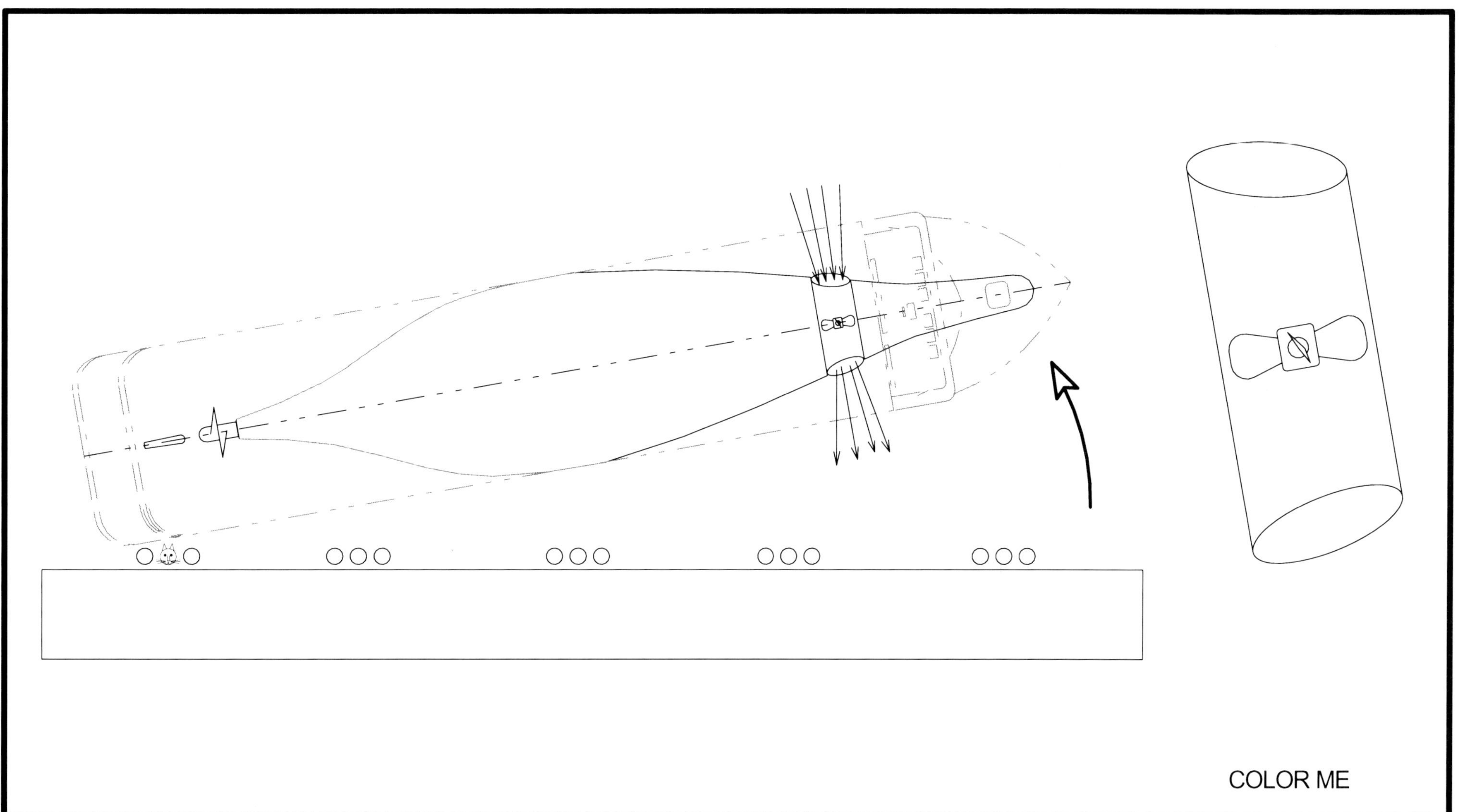
COLOR ME

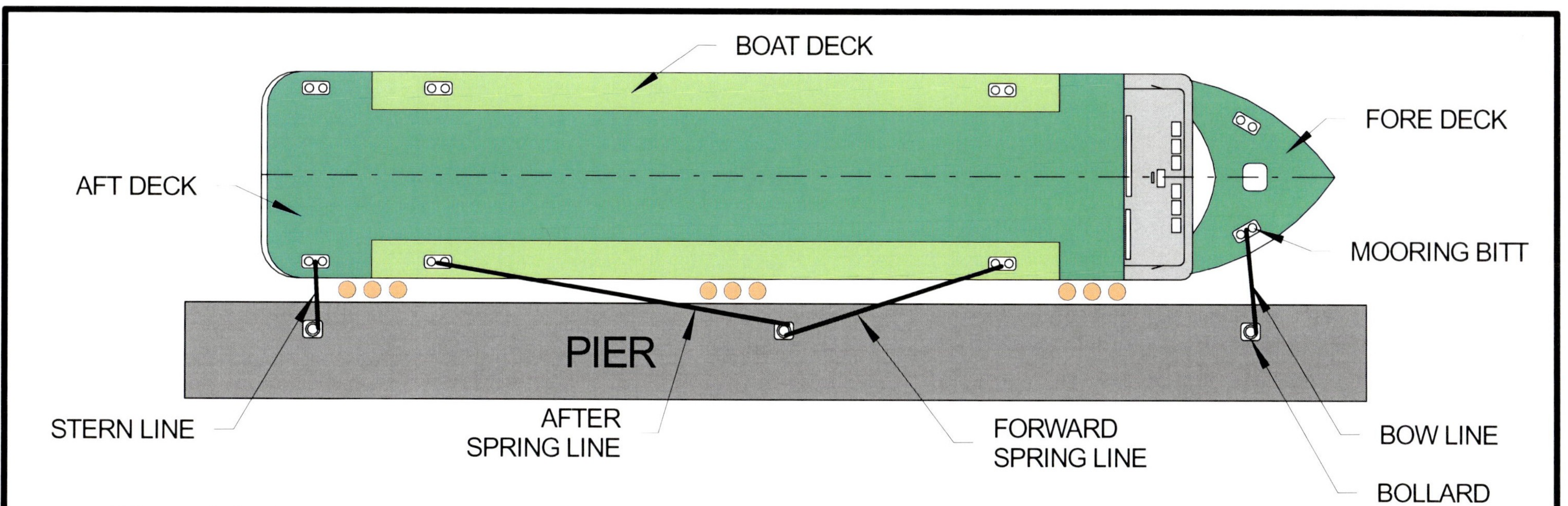

The ship is moored or tied up to the pier using heavy ropes called hawsers. Each hawser has a name.   The stern line keeps the stern tight against the pier. The bow line keeps the bow tight against the pier.   The forward spring line keeps the ship from moving forward, and the after spring line keeps the ship from moving aft.   The hawsers are attached to the mooring bitts on the ship and to the bollards on the pier.

MOORING OR TYING UP THE SHIP AT THE PIER

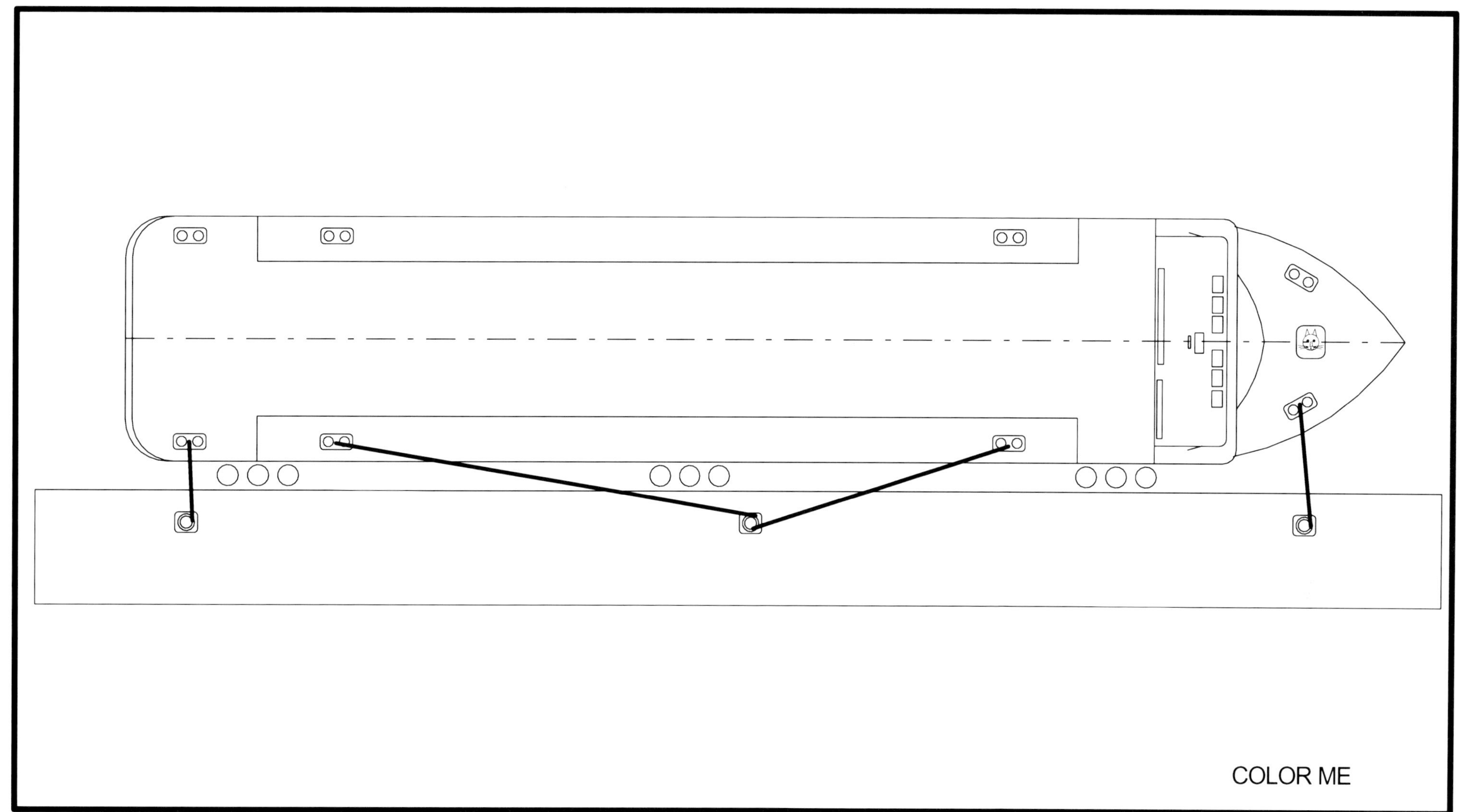

COLOR ME

This is a mooring bitt on the ship.

A mooring line is attached to it by winding it around the two posts.

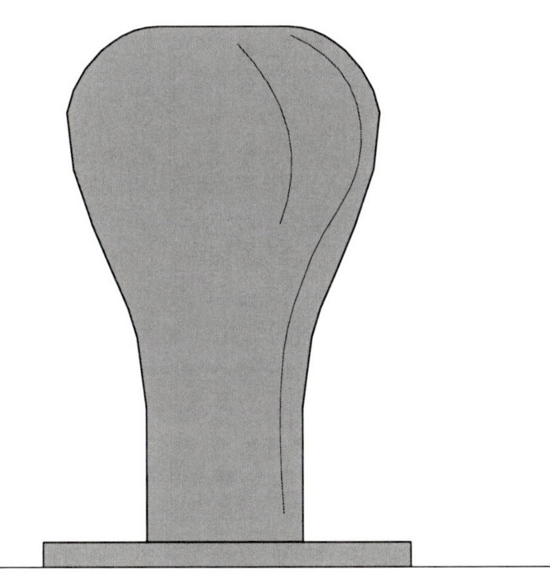

This is a bollard on the pier.

A loop or "eye" on the shore end of the mooring line is dropped over the bollard.

THE DIFFERENCE BETWEEN A BITT AND A BOLLARD

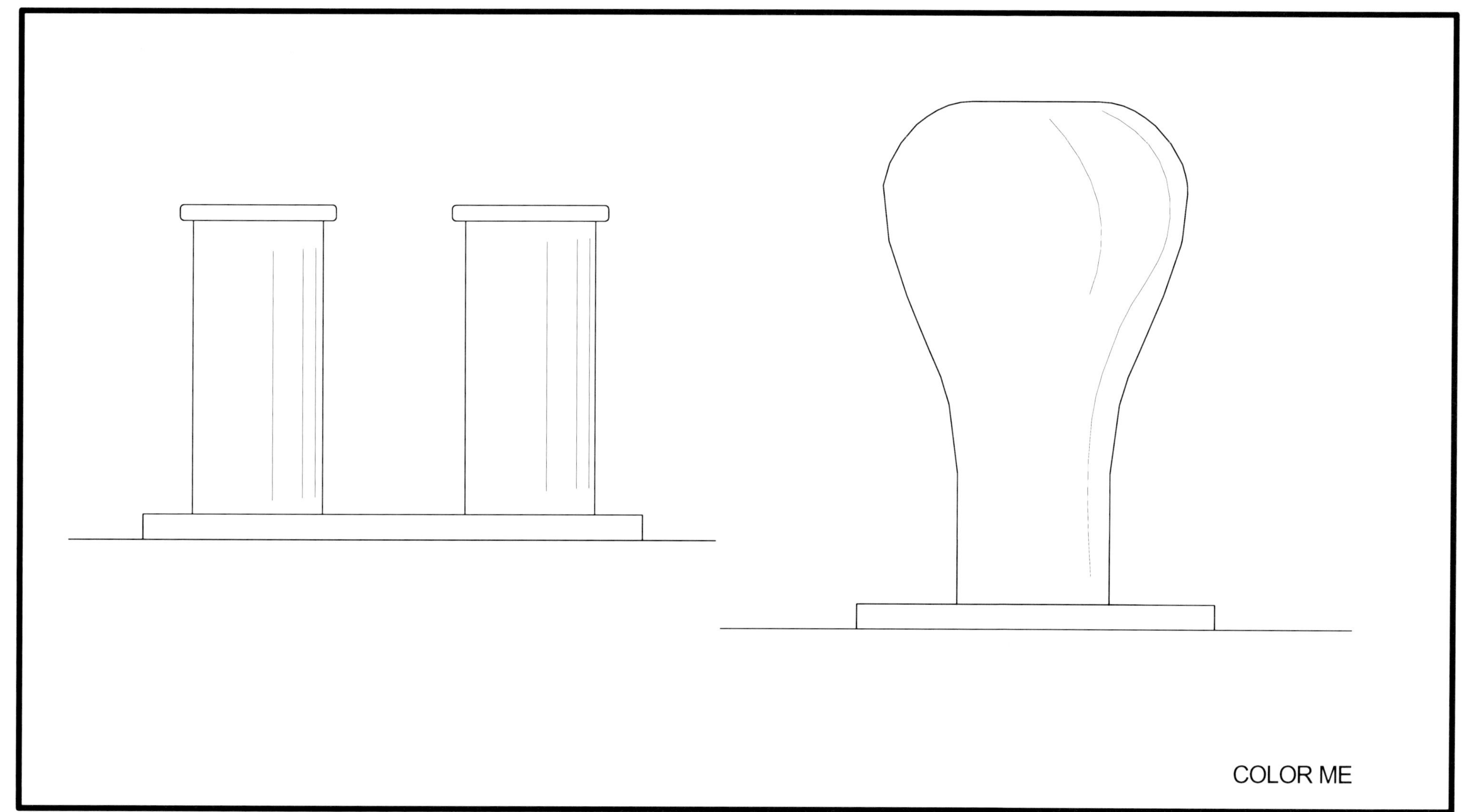

COLOR ME

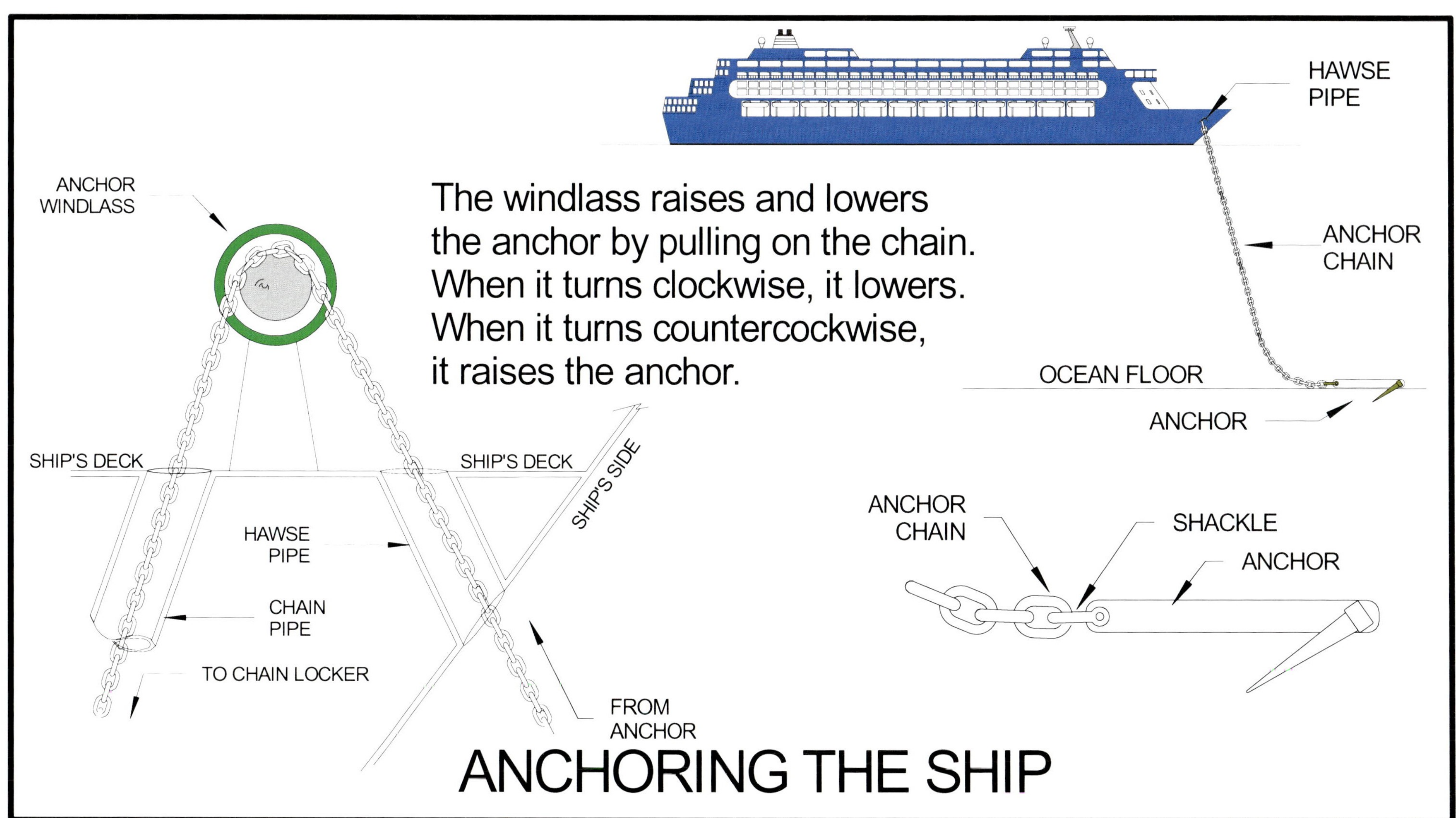

The windlass raises and lowers the anchor by pulling on the chain. When it turns clockwise, it lowers. When it turns countercockwise, it raises the anchor.

ANCHORING THE SHIP

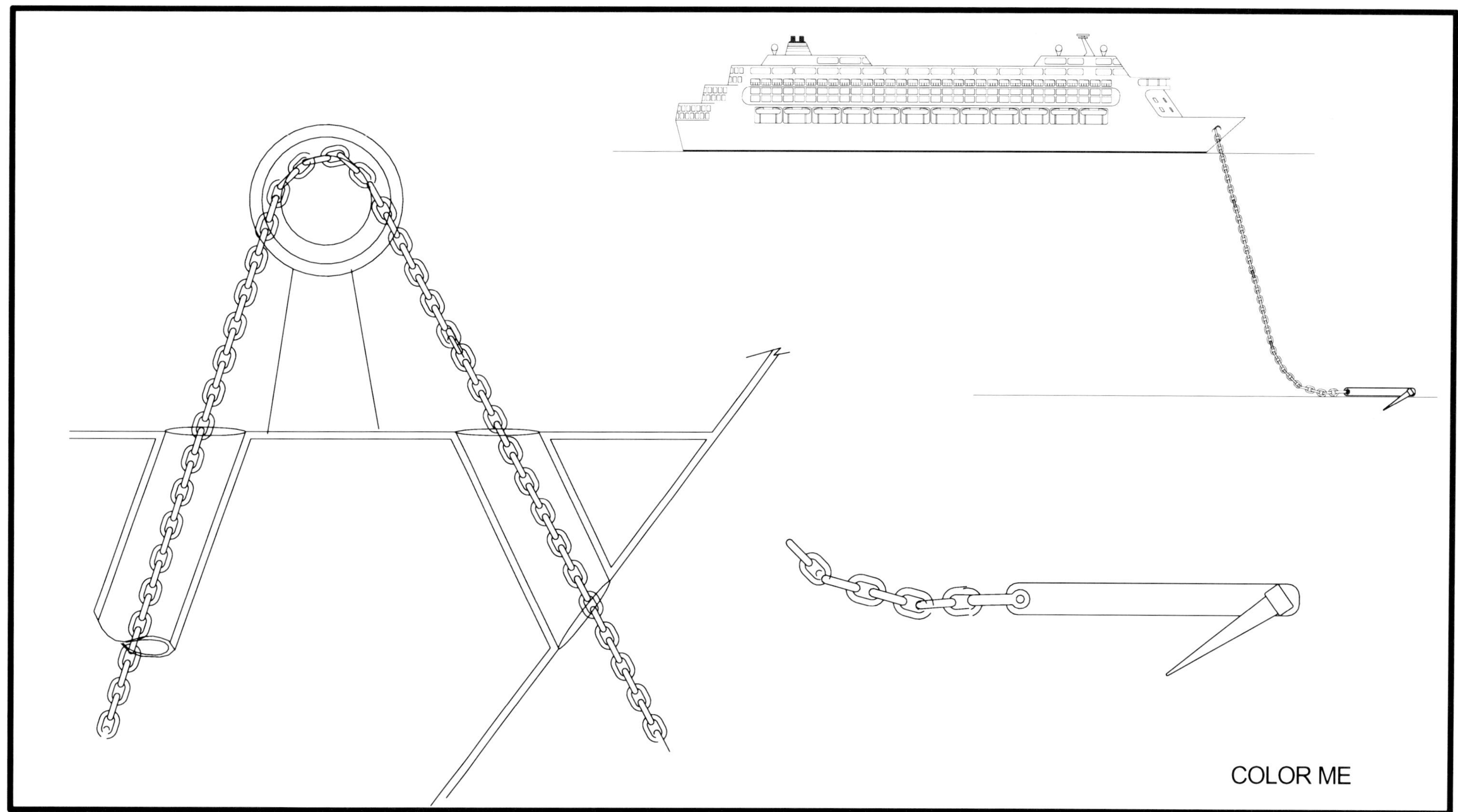
COLOR ME

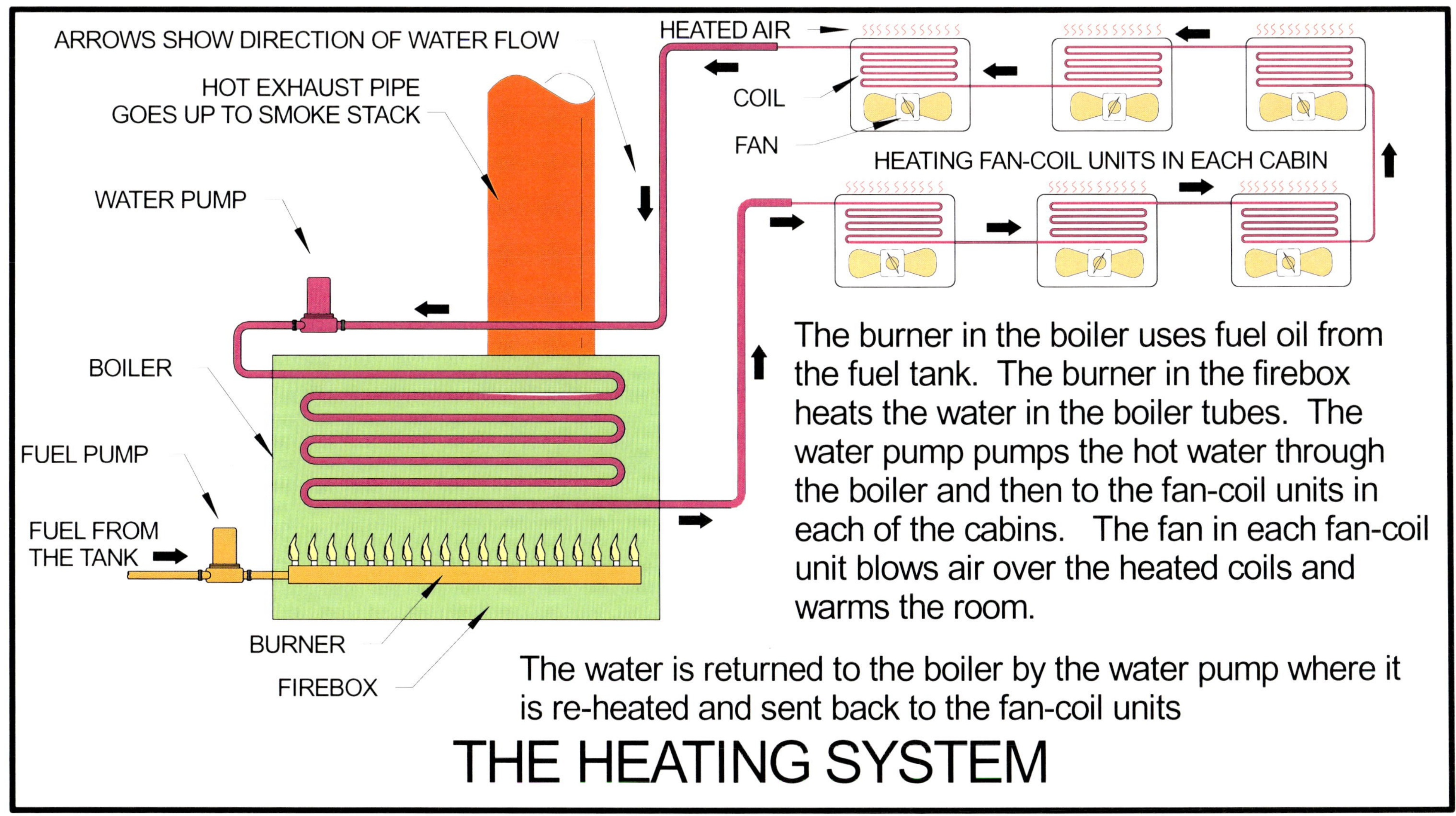

ARROWS SHOW DIRECTION OF WATER FLOW
HEATED AIR
HOT EXHAUST PIPE GOES UP TO SMOKE STACK
COIL
FAN
HEATING FAN-COIL UNITS IN EACH CABIN
WATER PUMP
BOILER
FUEL PUMP
FUEL FROM THE TANK
BURNER
FIREBOX
The burner in the boiler uses fuel oil from the fuel tank. The burner in the firebox heats the water in the boiler tubes. The water pump pumps the hot water through the boiler and then to the fan-coil units in each of the cabins.   The fan in each fan-coil unit blows air over the heated coils and warms the room.
The water is returned to the boiler by the water pump where it is re-heated and sent back to the fan-coil units
THE HEATING SYSTEM

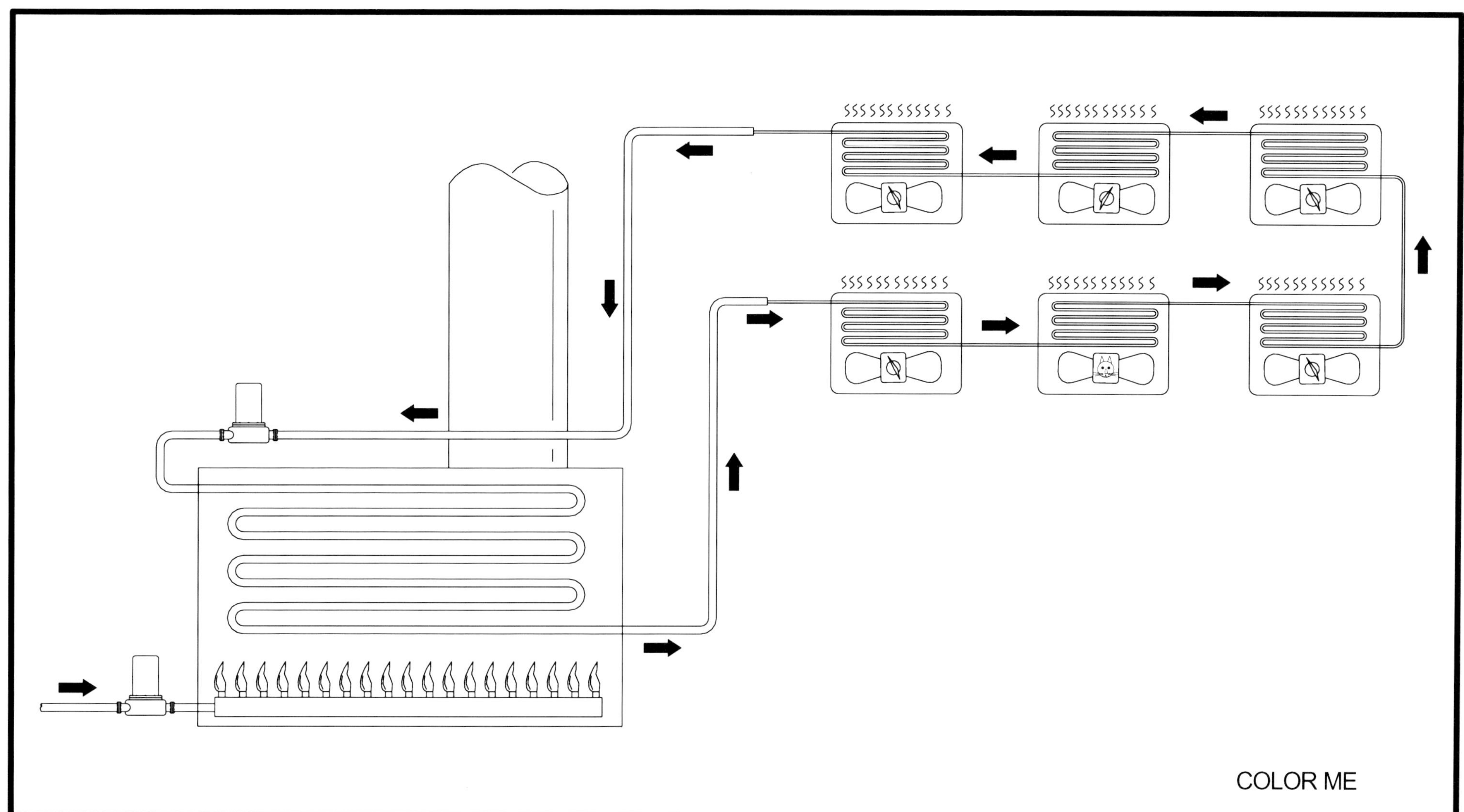

COLOR ME

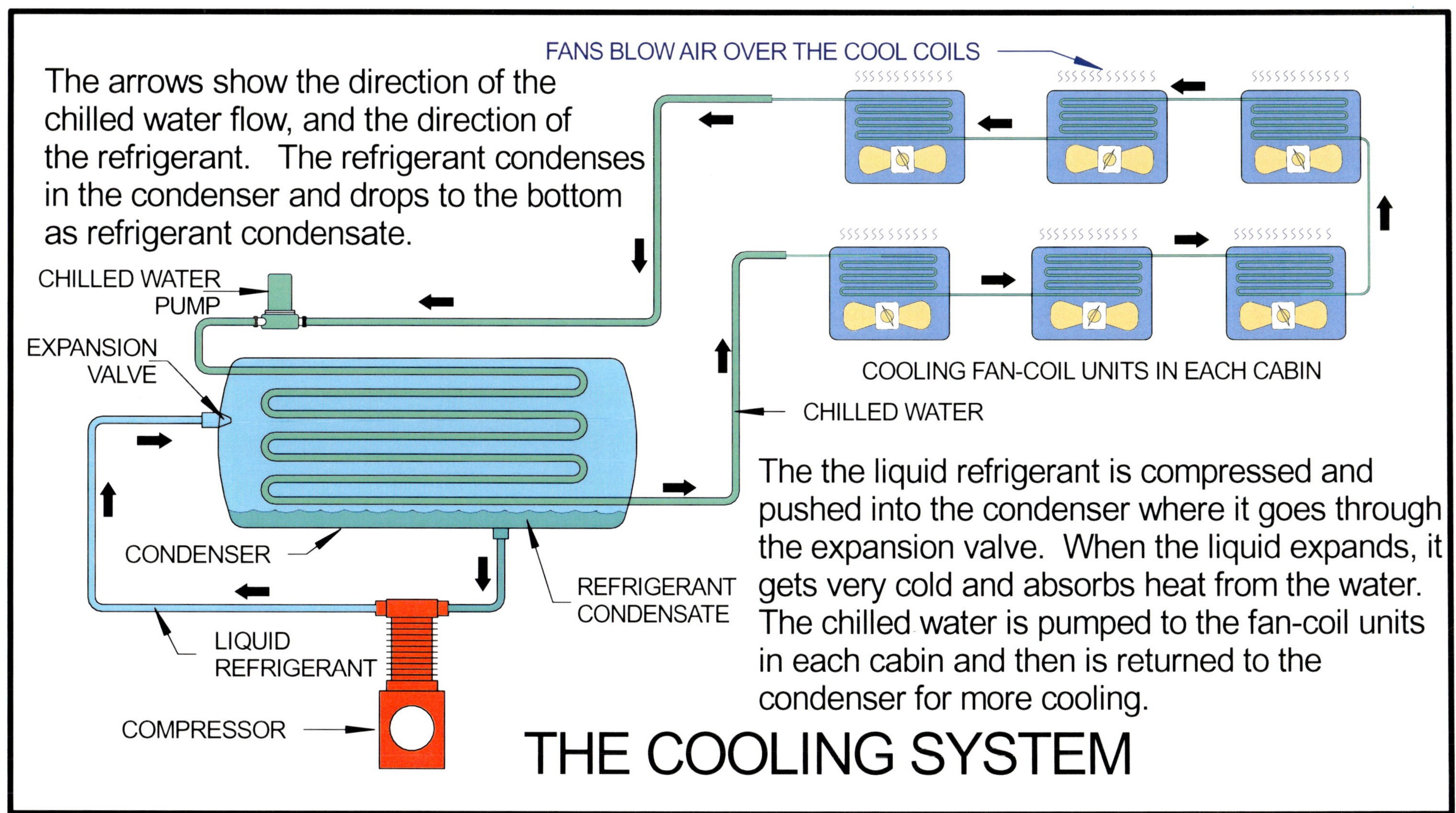

FANS BLOW AIR OVER THE COOL COILS
The arrows show the direction of the chilled water flow, and the direction of the refrigerant. The refrigerant condenses in the condenser and drops to the bottom as refrigerant condensate.
CHILLED WATER PUMP
EXPANSION VALVE
CONDENSER
LIQUID REFRIGERANT
COMPRESSOR
REFRIGERANT CONDENSATE
COOLING FAN-COIL UNITS IN EACH CABIN
CHILLED WATER
The the liquid refrigerant is compressed and pushed into the condenser where it goes through the expansion valve. When the liquid expands, it gets very cold and absorbs heat from the water. The chilled water is pumped to the fan-coil units in each cabin and then is returned to the condenser for more cooling.
THE COOLING SYSTEM

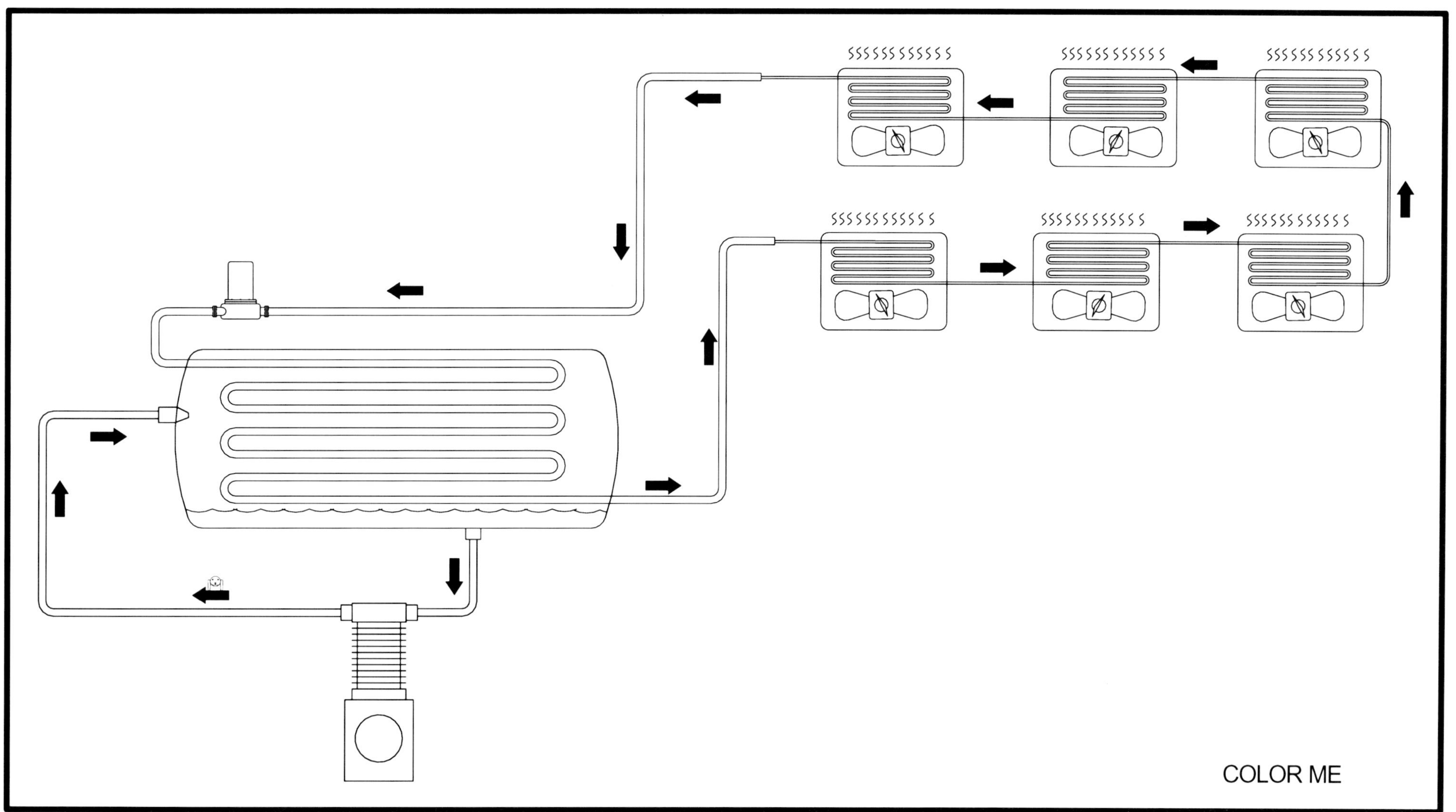
COLOR ME
60

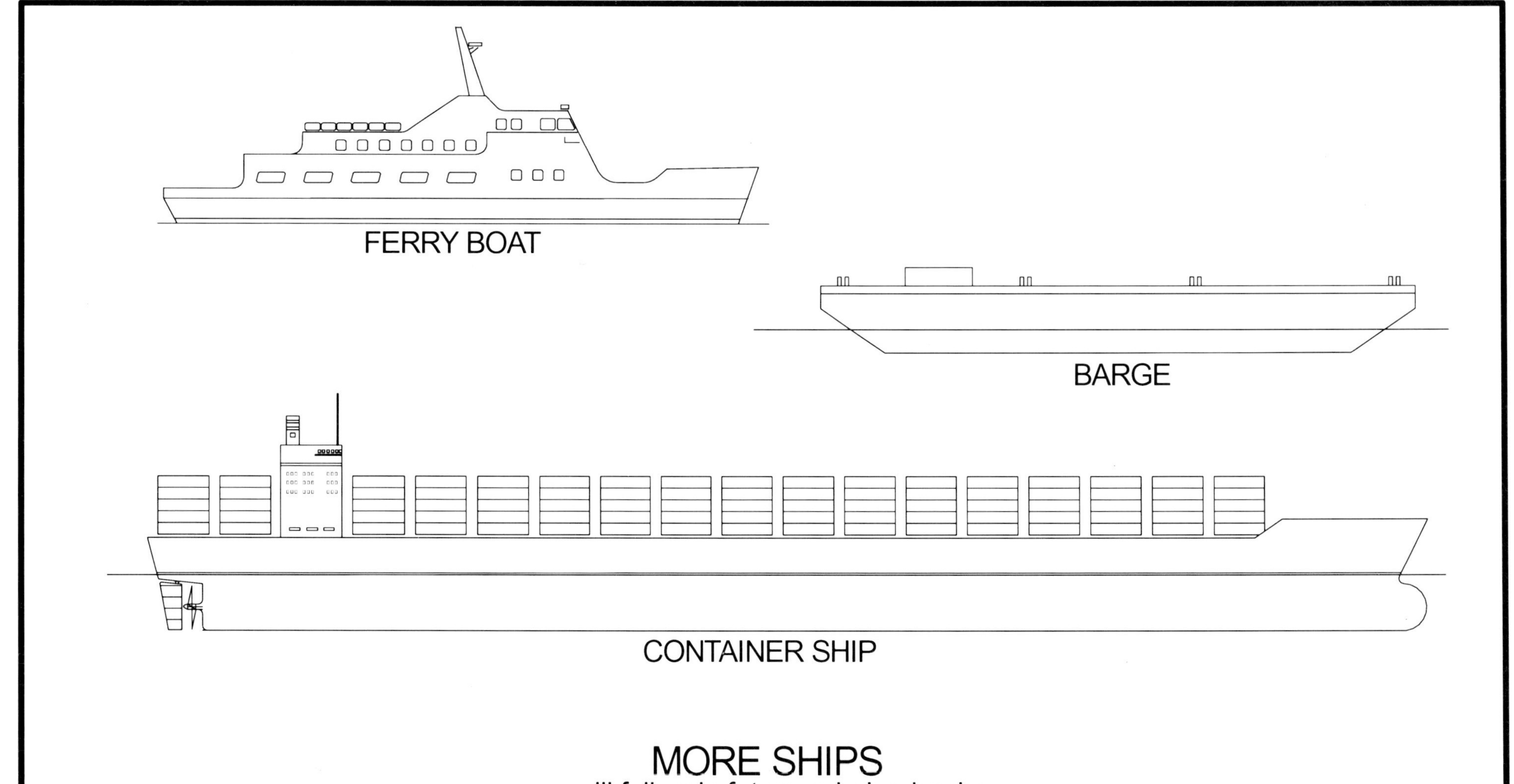

MORE SHIPS
will follow in future coloring books.